Maly Danino, PhD

# Coach Your Child to Success

Maly Danino, PhD

# Coach Your Child to Success

A Guide for Parents of Children

With Learning Disabilities and ADHD

**Contento De Semrik**

Maly Danino, PhD

**Coach Your Child to Success**

A Guide for Parents of Children
with Learning Disabilities and ADHD
Co-Author: Sivan Haft-Naftali

Senior Editors and Producers: Contento De Semrik

English Version: Haim Nissan Haviv
English Edit: Sigrid Macdonald
Hebrew book editing and production support: Goals Institute Ltd.
Design: Ilana Lasri
Hebrew book cover design: Keren & Golan | Graphic Design Studio
Cover Design: Yael Rosen | www.yds.co.il



ISBN: 978-965-550-116-2

International sole distributor:
Contento De Semrik
22 Isserles, 67014 Tel-Aviv, Israel
Semrik10@gmail.com
www.Semrik.com

# Table of Contents

# Preface

Along my professional path over the years, I have met many parents who conduct themselves in various ways in relation to their child. I have experienced the uncertainty with them at the start of the journey, the fears and apprehensions, the helplessness resulting from their attempts to cope with the educational and welfare bureaucracies – as well as the feelings of hope, of accomplishment and of success. The parents' willingness to meet and share with me a segment of their journeys, to allow me to walk by their side and accompany them on steep pathways and to be with them at certain crossroads where they had to make decisions, helped me to better understand their needs, the range of emotions they experience, and the complex means of coping required of the family in general and the parents in particular.

Many parents had approached me after having tried many solutions offered them, such as behavioral therapy or psychological treatment. Many felt that such treatments take too long and, in the end, are of little use in solving the difficult dilemmas and daily struggles they were facing, that as solutions, they were much less effective than they had anticipated. There were parents who shrunk from these solutions for they felt that they are not only interested in understanding the reasons for the difficulties they are facing, but also in seeking assistance that would be focused on solutions and effective results.

I made the decision to transform the meeting with parents, and their unique and tender touch to my heart, into a distinct *work plan* that would serve as a model for them to develop a sense of being that is self-able, thus allowing them to cope effectively with the challenge of being a parent to a child with learning disabilities.

The coaching ideas I was exposed to: positive thinking, focusing, mission-orientation and action – all these seemed fitting to me for the working model I sought to construct. I thought that this answer would provide the parent with more and better tools for coping more effectively, but more importantly, that it would instill in them a sense of being the masters of their own fate, and that they could mold their lives and direct themselves toward the fulfillment of their dreams and the empowerment of their children.

The moment I was able to conceptualize, for myself, the way I could attempt the intervention and offer mission-focused accompaniment which would, at the same time, be sensitive and attentive to, as well as aware of, the attributes of the difficulties the parents undergo, my thoughts and feelings caught fire.

This book directs the parent within, allowing him to reacquire himself, enabling him to better understand his feelings. It helps him see his child and his scene. Through questions which the parent asks himself, he attains new insights that assist him in forming a different and authentic approach, as opposed to externally directed ideas. When a parent succeeds in being self-attuned he learns to hear all his current-self thoughts, desires and dreams and facilitates a lucid vision of his genuine self. This state allows the parent and child to experience interaction and intimate bonding that will accompany them along the way in moments of greater and lesser joy.

This book will serve as a means of self-help for the parent – for it can be read more than once, each time exposing the parent to other and further layers, leading him to further insights, since even the parent is no longer at the same place he previously occupied; after all, "you can never enter the same river twice."

# Thanks

I am first and foremost grateful to Ofra Elul, Chairperson of the Nitzan Association for Children and Adults With Learning Disabilities in Israel, for her support and encouragement in the process of developing the models designed to bolster parents and children. I thank her for the partnership along the way and her heart's wisdom, thanks to which we have been successful in rallying Nitzan toward the objective it was established to accomplish.

Likewise, I feel gratitude to Nitzan's staff operating the coaching program headed by Anat Katznelson, who performs her mission tirelessly, in her endlessly dedicated way and with so much love.

A special thanks goes to Sivan Haft-Naftali who, by employing her unique approach, re-wrote and edited the raw materials. She was my right hand all along the way. This book could not have been written without her important and professional contribution.

I am thankful to my teachers and instructors throughout the

years, and especially to Professor Zippi Shechtman who opened a window for me into the emotional world of parents and children.

Special thanks are due the parents who agreed to share with us the moments of crisis and difficulty as well as the moments of hope and pride. Their stories are weaved into the book's tapestry and work to greatly enrich it by demonstrating, in a tangible form, the complex reality that parents must cope with.

Finally, I would like to express my love to my children – Inbal, Dvir and Or, who taught me, and still do day in and day out, the meaning embodied in the never-ending, existential experience of "being a parent."

# Introduction

The desire for parenthood has embedded in it an expectation and a promise of a better future and continuity. In many instances, the child is perceived by his parents as an opportunity and occasion for the fulfillment of dreams and manifestation of hopes and deeply held aspirations. Many parents endeavor to afford their children to go through a wide variety of activities in order to promote the acquisition of knowledge and a variety of tools from a very early age that will serve them later in life. This is done on the basis of an assumption that such would serve as a prerequisite for their growth and which would utilize the fulfillment of their dreams and aspirations.

Against this background, the word combinations: 'a child with learning disabilities' and 'parents of children with learning disabilities' are particularly loaded ones that might evoke a variety of feelings, situations, fears and apprehensions.

It is not an easy task to be the parent of a child with learning disabilities, or one with an *attention deficit hyperactivity disorder* (ADHD). In many cases, already in kindergarten the clash between the parent's desires and expectations and the painful reality in which, in most cases, the developmental differences among children become distinctly apparent.

Approximately, one in ten children is expected to develop differently than his peers, in other words, he will be less alert than his peers, less attentive, he will not be able to accomplish such tasks as cutting with scissors, using glue or painting and drawing with the same accuracy as other children, and might have difficulty with listening. While some of the children will be defined as having normal developmental delay, where later maturation of brain mechanisms could reduce the gap between them and their contemporaries and to a normal functioning later on in life, a different group, however, will experience significant difficulties that will just be amplified as the demands placed on them increase. The hardship entailed in the acquisition of a seemingly simple proficiency – such as the ability to read, write, add and subtract, skills acquired effortlessly by their peers – often stands in obvious contrast to well-acquired cognitive abilities and thus may bring about much frustration that will mushroom into social and emotional hardships.

## Social and Emotional Effects

Negative feelings, such as frustration, disappointment, failure and despair, flood the child due to his inability to perform various tasks, perceived as effortless for other children in his age-group. As time goes by, such emotional consequences could cause significant harm to the perception of the child's self-image, cause him to feel worthless and impair his ability to sufficiently integrate into the social setting of his peer-group.

A survey conducted by the Nitzan Association,[1] examined the perceptions of a number of parents as to the manner their children cope socially and emotionally. Fifty percent of parents of children with learning disabilities or ADHD reported the presence of such emotional hardships during the previous year. In comparison, only 16 percent of parents of children without learning disabilities reported such manifestations. A significant gap was also discovered between children with learning disabilities and those without on the social plateau: twenty-seven percent of parents with at least one child with learning disabilities or ADHD reported the existence of social maladaptation – as compared to only eight percent of parents to children without disabilities. From parents' accounts it turns out that at least 80 percent of children diagnosed with learning disabilities and/or ADHD received no information or guidance from school about the disability of their child. About two-thirds of these parents did not even meet during the year with professionals at school (such as educational counselors, school psychologists and the like), and most of them were displeased with the responses the school provided for the social and emotional difficulties experienced by their children.

A child with learning disabilities is involved in various social systems and not in all of them does he feel confident enough to give expression to the hard feelings he undergoes. In many instances the feelings of frustration, despair, failure and disappointment will come out mainly at home, where the child feels safe and protected. At home, the child feels that his place in

1. Conducted by the Smith Institute (Israel) in cooperation with Iris Kalka, PhD (June 2010).

the social structure will not be degraded if he opts to express frustration, sadness or anger, indeed, he expects to receive support and comfort there. This set of expectations, hardships and aspirations makes coping by the family a particularly complex effort.

The behavioral manifestations in response to the children's emotional expressions vary greatly. There are children who withdraw inwardly and exhibit excessive sensitivity, while others might express their frustration more forcefully and find it difficult to curb their feelings. This latter group might rebel, quarrel with their peers; and in some cases, where steady empathetic and loving presence is missing, they might drop out of formal educational systems.

## Effect on the Family Structure

In families where one or more children struggle with learning disabilities or ADHD often greater parental intervention is required in the lives of the children, whether at home or, systemically, at school.

Experience gained through research indicates that a child's behavior cannot be assessed apart from the existing family dynamics, the communication between the parents, the interaction among the siblings and the distribution of chores and tasks at home – all these, are affected by the distress manifested by the child, his conduct and his difficulties. For this reason, the interaction among family members often becomes dysfunctional.

Problem-solving approaches and manners of decision-making serve the child as models of social learning which would reinforce existing behavioral patterns and either exacerbate or alleviate the hardships he is experiencing.

This dynamic manifests more intensely in some families where one of the parents had struggled, during his childhood, with learning disabilities or difficulties. In such cases, the parent's experiences get interwoven into the tapestry of family life and his child's existence in such a way that, at times, it becomes consequently harder to formulate identity segregation processes and to shape a parent-child relationship, that would otherwise promote growth and independence for the child.

## Parental Coping

Parents employ many and various approaches for coping with the child's disability. Naturally, no broad, general outline for all such families may be drawn. I will attempt to describe some of the manners utilized for such coping, however, note that several characteristics, at times contradictory, might exist concurrently in a single family.

Denial commonly occurs as a form of coping – especially during the initial stages following a diagnosis of the disability by professional agencies. Such parents might deny the existence of a problem and assign its manifestation to delayed development that, in time, will vanish of its own accord. We may presume that these parents would ignore the objective difficulties the child encounters and will expect and demand from him to function like his peers, disregarding the obstacles preventing him from doing so.

Denial receives any number of behavioral expressions, and its difficulty does not necessarily preclude seeking a diagnostic route, even the acquisition of proper treatment services. In such a case, the parents might attach little weight to the learning disability or tie it to the daily social and emotional struggle the child undergoes both at home and in school. Often, such denial stems from a sincere belief in the child's ability and his potential to advance and overcome these impediments. That notwithstanding, this coping posture lacks the acknowledgment and acceptance by parents of the objective obstacles that the child is facing, therefore, joint processing of the matter is absent and may bring the child to feel alienated from his environment, resulting in a sense of isolation.

Some parents have experienced confusion and uneasiness as they faced their child's difficulty and at times have exhibited anger and annoyance towards him. These parents may not have comprehended the nature of the difficulty and might erroneously interpret it as a lack of motivation or of mere laziness, and would persist in demanding from their child a level of functioning appropriate for children with no learning disability. Studies in this field indicate that often parents of such children, whether due to lack of awareness or because of denial, develop high level of expectations and set a high bar of demands which are simply unattainable for that particular child. These families might delay seeking diagnosis and some, without first diagnosing their child, might send him to receive a range of treatments, hoping – even if unconsciously – for a "correction" of the disability in such a fashion.

Another common approach is that of lowering expectations. These parents feel greatly disappointed when they receive the diagnostician's findings and gradually, their expectations slip as do the demands they place on their child. These children, who are aware of the hidden messages thus conveyed to them by their parents, respond in different ways. Some, out of despair, would give up and accept the extant situation; others, in order to preserve a favorable status quo, would avoid any attempt to meet complex challenges; on the other hand there is that group whose members would make additional efforts in order to prove their ability to accomplish beyond what is expected of them.

There are occasions where the parents' dealing with their child's learning disability is accompanied with guilt feelings – especially after the diagnosis is understood. There are times where the guilt is evoked due to family circumstances or the economic complications of the family, which make the parent feel that he or she is unable to invest sufficient resources in assisting his child; or, alternatively, that personal or genetic factors passed from the parent to his progeny are the cause of the child's disadvantageous situation. Such parent's emotional reaction might be very intense, disproportional to the actual situation and the daily challenges he is in fact facing. On occasion it is due to over-identification with the child and re-experiencing old trauma from the time he attended school.

Over-identification with the child could manifest in active management by the parent, who would turn to assisting agencies in order to understand the hurdles and the necessary means of support and coping. Conversely, it could manifest in a form of passive handling, i.e., the parent would be unable to function in a way that would promote his child's growth.

Actively involved parents might turn to a variety of therapists and organizations in their attempt to better cope with their child's difficulty, in order to save the child from the negative experiences of pain and heartache. Some, thus, would seek enrichment and counseling courses and even undergo re-training to become professionally qualified in the field. Through such active involvement, based on research and study, the parent reaches an in-depth level of insight and understanding of

his child's difficulties and feelings of the requisite empathy. In this way a bond is formed where the child feels understood and the presence is someone in his life he can rely on.
In contrast, there are parents, who due to over-identification with their child's daily struggles, would experience ineptitude and find it hard to actively cope with their parental challenges. In some instances, one can observe families where roles have shifted: the children took their parents' place in an attempt to protect the latter from the heartbreak that their difficulties aroused.

## Parental Coaching as an Effective Intervention

In English, the word 'coach' means both a carriage (as a noun) and to train (as a verb). On the surface, there is seemingly no relation between the two, however, an examination of the importance of each allows a deeper insight of what it is to train in the context of powerful intervention.
The use of the word 'coach' – in its meaning of "a carriage" – started in the 16th Century. Its source is the Hungarian word *kocsi* short for the term *sosci szeker* meaning "a wagon" from the Hungarian town Kocsi, which was located next to the main highway between the two large cities of Vienna and Budapest. Over the years, by way of borrowing, the word 'coach' acquired a new meaning: beginning in the middle of the 16th Century it received the additional meaning of 'training,' mostly in the connotation of sports activities; nowadays, it has come to signify a person who facilitates movement from one place to another – i.e., a form of personal training, but not limited to a sport-type activity. Like the carriage, a coach takes one from where one is, to where he wants to go, toward achievement with an agreed

upon goal. The carriage is a metaphor for the trainer who transports the passenger (trainee) to where he desires his arrival. This is a relationship of mutual responsibility.
The training is based on the concept that each human being has innate growth and evolution forces and developmental resources of his own. The fundamental supposition is that the trainee knows his destination and the purpose of the training is to promote his journey there. The coach's role is to assist the trainee to become attentive to his own desires and point out the sources of his empowerment, his strengths, and then assist him in channeling them toward intelligent activity in an advancement designed to achieve his goals and fulfill his vision.

## Coaching Parents at the Nitzan Association

The training is an intervention method that is focused on the parent, calculated to afford him individual support designed for those particular parent's needs and challenges in order to effect a change in his life and affect the functioning and management of the family, in general, and the child in particular.
Parents' training at Nitzan is a short-term intervention, where the coach accompanies the parent during a self-observation process. The training enables the parent to develop his abilities and self-confidence so that he can then implement new coping strategies and amplify his child's daily learning opportunities. The coach's role is to assist the parent in honing his skills and capabilities, to re-shape his behavioral patterns as he struggles with crises and conflicts, and bring about an improvement in the relationships of the various life (social) cycles of the parent. The goal of training is to effect a change and transform the parent-in-training, from feeling helpless and repeatedly expe-

riencing failure, to a place where he materializes success in an emotional state that would charge and nourish faith and hope in him, thus, setting a basis for creating a genuine dialogue with his child.

## The Theoretical Rationale of the Training Model

The model for training parents is based on the three-stage model developed by Dr. Clara E. Hill (Hill 2005) and has been adjusted to the unique characteristics and complex predicaments faced by a family of a child with learning disabilities.
Clara Hill's therapeutic approach is affected by psychoanalytical, cognitive and behavioral theories and includes reference to three levels of human existence: emotional, cognitive and behavioral. The model is based on the presumption that only treatment at all three levels could lead to a genuine change. It has a stage of exploration, a stage of insight and a stage of action. Based on Dr. Hill's method, our conduct in life is a product of the interaction between our inborn personality, the experiences we go through and the experience we accumulate in life. Since it is not possible to alter formative life experiences from our past, or the basic temper we were born with, we ought to focus on the development of more adoptive emotions, thoughts and behavioral patterns.
In line with the three layers of the emotional, cognitive and behavioral patterns, the goal of training derived from this conceptualization is to lead a parent through a process of ascertaining his emotions, heightened awareness of the difficulties and undertaking the requisite changes in his life. All three stages are equally essential in structuring the process. The first stage lays the foundation for the two that follow and is the

blueprint of the insights to come, and in the same fashion, the stage of action is founded on deep insight of the difficulties and the need to provide assistance in order to help the parent advance toward action from the insights he has gained.
This diagram illustrates with greater clarity the theoretical model just presented:

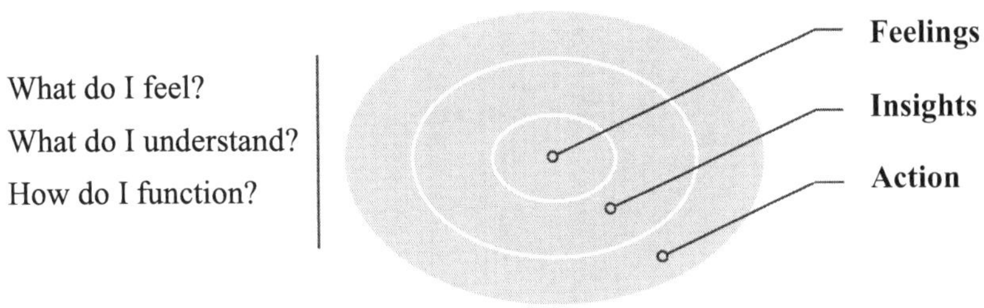


## The Three-Stage Model of Dr. Clara Hill

### 1. Exploration Stage

At the heart of the training model is the exploration of emotions and their processing. Processing emotions offers the parent-in-training the opportunity to express his feelings and to transform them with the help of the coach, thus reinforcing in him the sense that there is someone who understand him. This stage enables the parent to arrive at new insights and develop expanded consciousness toward the situation, so that in the future he will be able to cope with his tasks in a different and more effective manner.

At this stage the therapeutic relationship between the coach and the parent-in-training gets established, and becomes imbued with the quality of trust, understanding and sympathy. The coach's role is to promote growth-enhancing processes through the development of such emotional skills as awareness, balance and emotional sublimation by the parent-in-training. The coach should encourage the parent-in-training to share his story, as he experiences it, and to examine his thoughts and feelings out loud. The coach serves as a mirror that reflects the parent-in-training's inner feelings, in a manner that liberates the latter of the burden of defenses and blocks within him, which accompany the daily inner-thinking manner of the parent-in-training.
The coach is charged with the task of establishing an open and frank environment that would accompany the process throughout. Through nonverbal responses – expressing interest and attentiveness, repeating some of what is being said, reflecting emotions and asking open-ended questions – the coach manifests attentiveness and becomes aware of the parent's view of the situation.
The coach is saddled with a weighty responsibility, requiring a sensitive approach, one that is careful, respectful and precise. A skilled coach will not compel his ideas or imagery on the parent-in-training, instead, he will express empathy, hoping that in doing so it would aid him in understanding and, without apprehension of any kind, to get in tune with his inner voice.

## 2. The Insight Stage

At this stage, the parent and the coach work together in order to reach new insights regarding the parent-in-training's inner world. The purpose of these insights is to assist the parent-in-training to comprehend the causes of his conduct, feelings, and emotions. Such insights would allow him to restore a sense of control over his life and might serve as a re-organizational framework of new experiences in his everyday life. In this way, the parent-in-training would be able to reinterpret, in a way that differs from the usual, his life situations and aims, to regulate his conduct in a way that matches the new insights and concepts that he acquires.

Feedback and reflection of the parent-in-training's behavior, provided by the coach, is of great importance. Such feedback, and the conversation that consequently evolves, forms a tool in the hands of the coach to allow him to reach deep and inquire into the parent's patterns of behavior and its mechanisms and the factors that motivate related actions. Such feedback serves as a mirror for the parent-in-training which reflects for him the manner in which the environment, coach and others comprehend and interpret his conduct. This new viewpoint allows the parent-in-training to reexamine his thinking and behavioral patterns as a stage on his way to reformulate the requisite change.

The concept acquired at this stage is the basis on which the opportunity for change is founded. Therefore, this is a vital stage in the process and sometimes may be thorny and grueling for both the parent-in-training and the coach.

### 3. The Action Stage

During the third stage, the coach prepares the parent-in-training toward and through practical action that he will undertake. The action stage prepares the parent-in-training for entry into

*The Gym* where he will train in changing the way he will cope based on the new insights he will have acquired during the second stage, as he relinquishes existing behavioral patterns which block and delay growth processes in his life.

Past experience shows that, even though new insights were acquired, a portion of the parents-in-training find it difficult to shift to the action stage. The reasons for the difficulty are many and varied and it is important to define them with clarity, using judgment-free sensitivity, so as to assist the parent-in-training progress along with the process.

Some of the parents-in-training lack the requisite skills for undertaking the changes needed. Thus, in addition, it is necessary to ascertain what additional proficiencies would be needed for these parents to obtain and to assist them in their acquisition and enhancement. Moreover, many parents-in-training find it hard to alter old habits and prefer to act using familiar ways and means. Some are also required to deal with unsympathetic reactions from significant others which are not supportive of changes that are occurring.

The coach has the responsibility to examine the personal needs of the parent-in-training as well as the environmental pressures he is subjected to and outline the training process accordingly. The work process involved is very dynamic, and cooperative effort by the coach and the parent-in-training is mandatory. During the process, a constant evaluation of the parent-in-training's feelings takes place in light of the new aspects of a given quandary, together with the structuring of insights and solidifying the modification and course of action chosen. During such evaluation, brainstorming and the discovery of alternative forms of action or of skill acquisition may be had, in order to make the process appropriate, retrofitted for the needs and abilities of the parent-in-training. The training process at hand is neither linear nor rigid and should tolerate flexibility as it moves back and forth among its various stages.

## About the Image and Function of the Coach

Training is a thoughtful process – an art if you will. Its essence is embodied in the art of knowing when, how, how much and why. Its success depends on the coach's ability to finely measure the quantity of a specific training to the particular parent-in-training, the stage he has reached in his development towards the desired optimum and the growth potentialities that may be available at any given moment. The parents-in-training need assistance in conceptualizing their feelings with the most precise and applicable words, and the coach would assist them in becoming aware of certain experiences and in identifying the price they pay as a result of their progress-delaying behavioral patterns.

The coach is akin to a person holding a flashlight which – jointly with the parent-in-training – he illuminates the areas of progress they are about to move into. The skilled coach would assist to highlight future growth and development areas, which are realistically within reach for the parent-in-training, and offer missions that constitute a step forward from where the parent-in-training is at present. The importance of the quantity and timing of the training will also manifest in the choices made by the coach regarding what to share, what new information to teach and new skills to develop together with the parent-in-training's ability to benefit therefrom.

The coach enlists his feelings and intuition to figure out which stage the parent-in-training is at and which directions for progress he could engage in at each and every stage of development. At times the coach would feel that he should move rather cautiously when asking a question or responding to statements made by the parent-in-training, in other instances he would recognize the opportunity for a breakthrough and swiftly move forward. The inquiries and, sometimes, the parent-in-training's nonverbal responses assist the parent-in-training in focusing, and reaching greater depth in understanding new meanings of the situations he is struggling with at that juncture.

In many instances, the parents-in-training come into the process emotionally flooded which makes it hard for them to define a training goal that is separated from the emotional storm they are in the midst of. During their joint effort, the coach will assist the parent-in-training to relate to such emotional aspects in a manner that promotes growth by raising consciousness as to the other elements of the parent's self and by translating what he is experiencing into words. Thus, the coach helps the parent-in-training in replicating past and current experiences, in solidifying new insights and internalizing trials and challenges, reforming them as personal and continual narratives.

In this context, the ability of the coach to understand the parent-in-training and express empathy in relation to the latter's experiences and his struggles is an important tool in the training process. Many parents-in-training feel alone in their struggle with the challenges presented by parenthood to a child with learning disabilities, and find it difficult to believe that their difficulties can be comprehended and accommodated by others. The passage from and the bridging of despair to hope, shame to pride, anger to sadness and from animosity to love are made possible, among others things, as a result of respectful and fitting expression of empathy for the experience that the parent-in-training has been going through. The coach would endeavor to step into the parent's shoes and see the world as the former sees it, thus giving him the feeling of being understood. Empathy facilitates validation and acceptance; it softens the sense of isolation and consequently promotes the inquiry into the parent's subjective experience. A constant examination and reflection of whether the parent's words were accurately understood opens the door for further and new clarification of aspects, activities, experiences and feelings of the parent-in-training, allowing deeper and wider introspection, which would serve to promote the process as a whole.

## The Parent-in-Training/Coach Relationship

The relationship between the parent-in-training and the coach is critical to the training process. Accordingly, the coach must recognize both the forces that promote and those that hinder relationships in general and between him and the parent-in-training in particular.

One of the forces that promotes the training relationship is the coach's ability to be fully present for the other, to be focused on the existing strengths, opportunities and resources of the parent-in-training, while expressing faith, appreciation and respect to the path he is traversing. To be present means to listen with a different kind of attentiveness, one that is devoid of any preconceived ideas, one that gives all his attention to the moment – the joint encounter.

Opposite this positive force the coach's personal baggage might serve as a blocking factor that would delay the development of the interaction between the two. Naturally, as a human being and a professional, the coach carries with him the imprint of previous experiences, feelings he felt in similar situations, his own associative realm and beliefs and agendas he has formulated. All that notwithstanding, the joint working process has to be created out of current joint experiences of the two participants. The coach's ability to be fully and exclusively in the present moment – free from personal experience that is collateral to the activity, without his personal needs, training preconceptions, well-set positions or previous knowledge of the path and the messages – allows spontaneous and authentic reliance on the joint feelings and experiences of the coach and the parent-in-training. There is the provision of feedback that is in accord with the present experience of both participants that stems integrally from the intertwining bond that is being weaved from one moment to the next. Such special moments of the present can have tremendous influence on the relationship between coach and the parent-in-training and they can appreciably promote the whole process.

From an emotional perspective, from time to time a range of feelings is often evoked in the coach toward the parent-in-training, including: anger, boredom, rejection; as well as love for him and compassion is evoked in the coach – all these must be carefully and responsibly processed in such a way as not to damage the relationship and training. Processing and deep insight of such feelings may even be used as excellent raw material for additional study of the manner in which the parent-in-training had experienced his reality. The coach is solely responsible for apprehending his own feelings and emotions and coping with personal issues that might otherwise result in inappropriate responses.

## The Parent-in-Training During The Coaching Process

In the process of training, the parent-in-training gradually moves from the intuitive stage, i.e., the manner he usually acts (automatic pilot) – to the stage where he cognitively analyzes his mode of action: he puts a handle on his thoughts and feelings, takes apart the way he negotiates into its stages, and constructs the missions in a fashion that is fitting for him and his child.

Within the process' framework the parent-in-training learns to expand his ability to observe, to comprehend and feel his experiences and trials in a more clear-cut manner and, accordingly, to set for himself achievable goals and objectives. An important aspect of the parent-in-training's learning concerns his ability to implement the method of thinking he had acquired in training to new situations outside the training process, and consider even a minor success an opportunity to generate additional successes.

This is the place to note that at the start of training many parents assume that they know, understand and are familiar with the thoughts, desires, dreams and ambitions of their child; however, in many instances reality is at odds with this assumption, and the parents find it difficult to relate to it as it is experienced by their child. The parent's angle of observation is not only affected by the way he had experienced the family dynamics at present or his child's difficulties in other frameworks, but also by his own childhood experience. This perception of parents profoundly affects the relationship between the parent and his child as well as the child's behavior.

Based on the recognition of the parents-in-training's difficulty in disengaging from their past as children and the experiences of their childhood, use is made of this situation during training in reflection. Through reflection the coach encourages the parent-in-training to examine and expose the hidden events of his life in the past and the present, which rise to the surface in the decision making process in his daily conduct. This superior observation method is not easy for anyone and, naturally, most parents find it difficult to outline their pattern of behavior beyond the actual interaction in a particular situation. In the training process the coach assists the parent to examine in a different light the way he copes with the learning disabilities of his son or daughter. The parent is encouraged to bring up authentic examples from his life and describe them in minute detail. Such a process, guided by the coach but based on examples described by the parent, stirs the parent to acknowledge and crystallize new insights in relation to coping mechanisms that could serve him well. The joint road taken by the coach and the parent-in-training teaches the latter to observe and identify the hidden aspects of his behavior, which control his interaction with his child and often his life in other contexts.

One of the more important tools the process gives the parents is called *color separation.* In this procedure the parent learns to conduct a dialogue with is child avoiding preconceived ideas that contain a determination or judgment regarding his child, his experiences or feelings. The parent-in-training learns to allow himself to conduct a dialogue with his child from a curious and open position, as opposed to a rigid and unequivocal one, which facilitates acceptance of the child and his growth potentialities. Usage of color separation encourages a dynamic process that never ends. Through it, the child learns and discovers things he did not know about himself and is thus able to materialize more and more elements of the self while the parent-in-training gets to know his child more fully and completely.

Parents' training beckons a new and challenging journey along a path never traveled before by the parent and child. The training process is designed to assist the parent-in-training to reformulate his way of thinking and coping and to assist in, even if indirectly, the internalization of better enabling coping mechanisms in his child's life. This process is based on the supposition that what takes place during training has parallel manifestations, in other words, what the parent went through with the coach, his child will undergo with him, at home. The working assumption is that the discourse between coach and parent during these encounters serves as a model for a corresponding discourse between parent and child. Therefore, while the coach enables the parent to look within, as he serves as a guide for him – likewise, the parent would enable his child to look inwardly as they conduct an in-depth, interior and essential dialogue, that forms a human-emotional bond between them that promotes growth and activity. The coach empowers, energizes and inspires the parent-in-training so that he could duplicate the process with his child. The expectation is that the child will be directly affected, and that the parent will become the 'coach-parent' of his child.

## Maintenance of Coach Fitness & Qualifications

The training process lays a great responsibility on the coach: he must conceptualize in a cognitive manner the process the parent-in-training goes through and, correspondingly, be aware of the experiences and feelings the parent-in-training goes through while shaping and nurturing an open, empathic, accommodating and encouraging dialogue that would enable the establishment of a secure and protective environment for the parent. Such an environment would stimulate the parent-in-training to search for and ascertain his behavioral patterns and beliefs and concurrently encourage him to seek and accomplish his training goals.

The complexity of the interaction and the dynamics of forming the association, which is designed to fit the needs of the parent-in-training, require deep self-awareness, high-level training skills and cognitive and emotional flexibility. Naturally, the coach brings with him to the interaction and the relationship being weaved with the parent-in-training his own beliefs, tendencies and temper, that do not always harmonize with those of the parent-in-training.

The process by which the coach hones his professional ability and develops his attendant thinking includes his commitment and responsibility to be trained by other coaches. The training encounters might awaken inner, stormy feelings within the coach's psyche, however, awareness and emotional insight of oneself would serve to regulate and sublimate them. The parallel training process aids the coach in processing the challenging experiences that rise from training the parent-in-training; likewise, it assists him in investigating and understanding his own thinking and behavioral conduct. Just being in a parallel process – as coach and trainee – enables the coach to polish his interpersonall skills, get deeper understanding of the interpersonal processes and allows more meaningful interaction with the parent-in-training that fosters growth.

## Book Structure: A Series of Encounters Between Coach and Parent

**During the First Encounter**, coach and parent become acquainted with each other. The coach ascertains the nature of the main difficulty of the parent's child, the reasons that brought him to the process and what are his expectations therein as he focuses on previous interventions to date.

**During the Second Encounter**, the parent-in-training is asked to visualize in his mind a future picture of his child. Thus the parent is motivated by the 'here and now' to envision a realistic future picture anchored in current reality as he experiences it. In addition, the parent-in-training experiences exercising a minor, achievable goal that would allow him to experience progress and success.

**During the Third Encounter**, the parent defines the first training goal following the dialogue he had held with his child. The coach assists him in choosing a modest and attainable objective that would allow him to experience progress and success.

**During the Fourth Encounter**, the parent-in-training shifts from defining an external training goal to outlining an internal one now based on objective reality leading to a change, even a barely perceptible one – as long as it is considered significant as it is experienced by the parent-in-training.

**During the Fifth Encounter**, the parent-in-training learns about himself: his strength, weaknesses, apprehensions, threats in his reality and the opportunities embodied in all these. Through stories taken out of his life, the coach brings the parent-in-training to meet both successes and failures he has been through, and enables him to understand that a given difficulty can serve as a challenge of great significance in the process of developing coping skills regarding his child.

**During the Sixth Encounter**, the parent-in-training enhances his awareness of the values guiding him in life, by presenting the following question: To what do I say "Yes," and to what do I say "No"? Thus, he develops insights that help him see both aspects of the value in which he believes, and comprehend that there are no absolute values.

**During the Seventh Encounter**, an assessment of the parent-in-training's progress is conducted. He is asked again to see a picture of his child in the future, then a comparison is conducted between the future picture he envisioned in the second encounter and the one envisioned in this one.

**During the Eighth Encounter** is where preparation for action is made. The parent-in-training and coach will plan a detailed process of reflection that would enable the coach to examine the training goal, its clarity, its focus on the child and his strengths as well as the needs of the parent-in-training and his strengths, and to examine to what extent the mission assists in the fulfillment of the child's future picture and expresses the empowerment model and values the parent wants to have his child acquire.

**The Ninth, Tenth and Eleventh Encounters** are training sessions (in *The Gym*). During these encounters the parent-in-training undertakes the performance of well-defined missions after he has completed the investigation stage and has developed new insights that would serve to maximize accomplishment of the training goal. Each encounter will be composed of the following stages: Planning, performance and learning improvement.

**During the Twelfth Encounter,** the coach will sum up the process by getting feedback from the parent-in-training that will allow himself to appreciate the significant events he had experienced and to examine in-depth what he has been through so far, the progress he has made to date, and his connection with the coach. The coach will share with the parent-in-training what he had seen and experienced during the training and will end with words of farewell.

**The Thirteenth Encounter** is a follow-up encounter that takes place six months after the training process had reached its conclusion. During this encounter the coach and the parent-in-training will examine the training accomplishments from the perspective of the time that has passed since training.

## First Encounter

# Getting Acquainted

During the first encounter we will get acquainted with the parent-in-training.[2] We will understand why he chose the procedure we are offering, and we will enter a training contract with him.
During this initial encounter we will identify two main issues that will facilitate the training process:

1. What is the child's main challenge?
   Our focus here will be on previous interventions both with the child and the parents; we will examine what has worked and what hasn't.

---

2. For convenience we will relate to the parent-in-training as a "he"; however, this pronoun is intended to refer to both genders.

2. What are the reasons that brought the parent to seek training? And what are his expectations of this process?

## Commencing the Encounter – Getting Acquainted

This encounter allows initial contact and a mutual introduction between the parent who is about to be trained and the coach. Sometimes, at the start of the encounter, the parent-in-training might find it difficult to express himself. It is, however, essential to enable him to form a free flow in expressing himself, without directing him.
If he should ask, *"Where do I start?"* the coach could respond, *"Wherever it suits you. Wherever you feel comfortable to start."*

## Naomi's Visiting Card

When Naomi arrived for training she presented herself thus:
*"I'm 50 and have three children. I've been married for 27 years already. I now work as a secretary in a law office. My oldest daughter works for an insurance firm. My second daughter is a high school teacher, and I have good relationships with both of them. I also have a 15-year-old son, and I have great difficulties with him at home. I feel guilty all the time. Today I read in the newspaper about parents who are alienated from their adolescent child, which is how I feel about my son."*

## The Coach's Card

At this juncture we will introduce ourselves and present our "business card." We will impart information about us and share with the parent-in-training information on our professional experience. We will emphasize our work with parents who are coping with their children's learning disabilities and/or attention deficit disorder.

We could say: *"I've listened to what you've told me and I'm grateful for your sharing with me. I'm looking forward to our future meetings with both anticipation and interest. I'm also anticipating the journey we will travel together. As a parents' coach of the Nitzan Association I believe in the significance and ability of the parents to materialize a change in their children's life. We will undertake a joint journey of empowerment, self-examination and you getting in touch with your own strengths and capabilities. It will be an adventure of sorts, a unique experience, different than anything you have experienced to date."*

## Importance of the First Encounter

Most parents arriving to receive training have already been through many situations in their lives and have done much for their child. Despite their massive efforts, these parents arrive at the first encounter with a feeling of helplessness and frustration. It is to be expected that they will arrive angry, exhausted and feeling saturated.

This encounter is of critical importance, for in it the parent-in-training will arrive at this decision whether or not to proceed with the process of training. In large measure, the decision is based on the human bond that forms between the coach and the parent-in-training. This bond is a dialogue 'at eye level' that creates a junction of similar and dissimilar experiences that each has been through in life: pain, sorrow, joy and excitement. This is the juncture when the joint journey should commence.

## Parent Accounts[3]

*"I have had some very hard days, and I'll never forgive myself for the confrontations I got into ... that is, between me and her. This is a heavy burden of guilt ... and there are those times where you feel inferior and failing as a parent, and this emotional state diverts you, makes you go wrong, and you actually know that you are going down the wrong path."*

*"Sometimes I'd reach the point where I'd hug one of them so as to block the ... the hyper... this noise that forms in my head; it is to be always in a state of permanent disquiet. It saps your energy. It gnaws at you from the inside ... this utter lack of time for yourself – where do I find myself in all of this commotion? Where do I give myself a timeout?"*

3. From the book, *The Parent as a Coach* (Danino, 2007).

*"I failed to make the connection. I didn't understand, I got mad, I thought she was just lazy. It was a shot in the dark ... at first you don't know what has landed on you; you don't know where it came from, what it is, and where to start in order to deal with it."*

*"I didn't know how to define it ... you see the child deteriorating and you don't comprehend what is going on..."*

*"When the first diagnosis arrived I sat down and cried. The feeling of guilt and anger the ... this ... self-accusation of, 'How could I have been so demanding toward her – she wasn't at fault!' It's something that burdens you all the years. In retrospect, you realize that she was not able to do certain things. It's a form of a handicap."*

*"I want to acquire tools to cope with her, because all day long I am angry at her, I yell at her and demand things from her ... maybe she actually is unable to do what I request that she do? I need help."*

## Dialogue Between Coach and Parent

At this encounter, the dialogue between the coach and parent-in-training is a sort of monologue of the parent; it is the role of the coach to ask leading questions, using them in order to direct the interaction. Remember: the parent-in-training is flooded with emotion; accordingly, it is important to allow the flow of his expression and avoid cutting him off.

## The Coach's Role in the Dialogue

This kind of a dialogue, where the parent-in-training speaks uninterruptedly, ceaselessly, might cause the coach to feel over-saturated. The contents rising do not leave the coach detached or aloof; indeed, he even comes across his own feelings. Amid such loaded dialogue, the coach has to be sensitive, empathetic and contain the parent-in-training's emotions on the one hand, and on the other hand remain objective, thus being able to see the reality with which the parent is contending through the proper perspective.

The role of the coach during the dialogue is to assist the parent in conceptualizing his thoughts and reflecting his feelings. He must locate those crucial footholds that will, later on, help bring order into what is verbalized in the process. These expressions will later serve as 'raw materials' in the course of training.

It is crucial that the parent feel that he has arrived at the right place, where he is neither judged nor criticized. In fact, this is the only encounter during which the coach will let the parent over-saturate him.

## Overcoming the Speaking Block

Sometimes, the parent-in-training finds it hard to talk and it is difficult to draw him out. By repeating the words he utters and asking questions aimed at expanding and deepening what has been said, it is possible to enhance articulation.

Thus, one can ask the parent questions that will encourage him to clarify and hone in on what he said. For instance, does he agree with the statement we just made? Was our expression accurate?

Getting the parent-in-training to verbalize allows him to hear himself, facilitates him to sort out and organize his thoughts, and allows him to conceptualize and surface the formed concepts to his awareness.

## My Child's Main Challenge

We will ask the parent-in-training: "**What is your child's main challenge, the one that made you come here for training?**"

We can assume that his answer will come out gushing in a rapid-fire mode, and that he will describe the great many difficulties that flood him at present.

The coach's role at this stage is to be present as the parent-in-training goes through his pain and frustration – and not to try and comfort him with such statements as: *"It'll be all right ..."*

## Jasmine's Obstacle

When Karen was asked what was the main difficulty her daughter had, the one that had caused her to commence training, she said:

*"Jasmine is a wonderful child. Charming, beautiful. She's 16 and she takes her adolescence to an extreme. She is flippant and rebellious, lazy, plays hooky from school every day. She constantly asks to be left alone. Every time we (the parents) confront her about it, it ends badly. Most often, we are compelled to give up and she comes out the winner. One time we asked her to stop surfing the Internet – she had an exam in History. We told her that if she would not quit, we'd disconnect the PC. In response, she said she would not go to school till we allowed her access to the computer. In the end we 'folded' and she got exactly what she wanted. Schooling was hard for her. When you sit with her one-on-one she's able to focus and does well, alone; however, there is no chance she'll sit and study, for she has no motivation. She can dawdle for hours doing nothing. We're doing everything in our power: private tutoring, we fawn over her and we constantly tell her how much we love her. We are constantly worried as to whom she hangs around with and whether she cares enough to be safe. We try to set clear boundaries for her; my husband is convinced that I've ruined her, that I give in too much, thus allowing her to do what she likes. I'm confused and don't know what to do. I'm stressed out all the time. I am constantly preoccupied with such thoughts as to where she might be and what is happening to her at*

*any given moment. I'd like to come to a point where I could sit quietly and just not worry, settle down and tell myself that soon it will all be over."*

## Danny's Hindrance

Yael arrived for training because of Danny. She described his difficulties, which were mainly lack of tidiness and disorganization, shifting from one task to another, difficulties in completing assignments, resident disquiet and outbursts of rage: *"Putting him to sleep is a war. To get him to shower, I have to beg him ceaselessly, and after he goes in I have to beg him to come out. His room looks atrocious and even when we arrange it for him, it rapidly re-assumes its former chaotic state. He constantly loses or forgets things. Lately, he even lost his cell phone and we (the parents) decided this time to teach him a lesson. We feel that we have to continually be on guard and watch him. We do not always agree between ourselves how to manage the problem. My husband thinks that I should not arrange his room: that he has to learn the hard way that there are no breaks in life. I disagree with him, 'cause we have learned from the diagnosis that Danny is not doing it on purpose. It's not his fault. We need tools and a roadmap so that we will not confuse him. In the past we attended marriage counseling, but its focus was on us. It did not give us the means to cope with Danny. This time I anticipate receiving some direction and acknowledgement regarding my way of doing things, and then maybe there is another way."*

## Curiosity & Discovery

Note, it is not just passive listening we are engaged in; we also inquire. We ask the parent-in-training to clarify, to enhance and to provide examples. We seek minute details by way of questions such as: *"Please explain what you mean by that."* Or, *"Give me an example,"* etc. The aim is to approximate an investigator who delves to the bottom of the meaning of the parent's words; we will constantly be in a state of curiosity and discovery. We will endeavor to experience the parent-in-training's story, to study his story and get to know him.

## To Know How to Listen

Through the parent-in-training the coach re-encounters his own past experiences which, on the one hand, help him bond with the parent-in-training, be empathetic and sensitive to his state – but on the other hand, could blur the uniqueness in the parent-in-training's account.

The coach must be completely attuned to the parent-in-training and remind himself: *"Even though the events or feelings resemble those I have experienced, it is not necessarily familiar ground."* The coach must hear the narrative as if he is hearing it for the first time – and not allow his thoughts and feelings to color his perception with his own, familiar experiences.

It is important in our interaction with the parent-in-training to avoid perceptual simplicity regarding what is said. Instead, we should try to listen to the subtext. It is necessary for us to understand that we do not have all the answers, and that we raise questions all the time.

We could, for instance, ask ourselves:

- What did he actually convey to me in that particular sentence?
- What did he mean?
- What does his assertion mean to him?

## Reasons & Expectations

We will ask leading questions, whose purpose is to clarify and refine the underlying reasons leading the parent-in-training to seek training in the first place. We could do it through the following query:[4]

- **What are the reasons that brought you to seek training?**
- **What are your expectations of the training process you are about to undergo?**

## Black & White in Lior's World

It was his 17-year-old son, Lior, who brought Nathan to seek training. Lior had learning disabilities and ADHD. He was diagnosed at a very early

4. See Navigation Sheet No. 1, p. 59.

age, and as a result of the extensive difficulties he had in childhood, he was treated by both a speech therapist and an occupational therapist.

It was difficult for Lior to cope with unfamiliar situations. When I asked Nathan why he sought training, he responded: *"It is difficult for me to contain him. It is hard to draw him out of his world, and it is impossible to compel him to do anything. He sees the world in black and white and his verbosity – getting into the most minute details – tires me. He has the capacity to argue about anything and everything as he is seeking ultimate justice. I am fatigued. His emotional state is that of a little child. Sometimes he behaves like a five-year-old, which causes me to feel lost. I don't know what to do and how to conduct myself."*

When the coach asked Nathan what his expectations were from the training process, he said: *"I expect a change. I want to know how to better cope, and to stop pulling solutions like rabbits out of a hat. I want him to have self-confidence and friends, so he does not feel lonesome. I want him be ready for the draft into the army.*[5] *I'm scared to death thinking what might happen to him there."*

## Restoring Peace & Quiet

Liora came for training because of her 12-year-old daughter, Almog, who was diagnosed as a gifted

5. In Israel, military service is still mandatory.

child with learning disabilities. Almog refused to do her homework. She sat in front of the TV for hours on end instead of studying for exams. Her difficulties started in the first grade. She was never able to copy materials from the board and was treated by an occupational therapist. Almog was very frustrated; mainly she could not understand why everybody else was able to copy the materials in time while she was unable to do so. When the coach asked Liora why she sought training, she said: *"Now that she's in the fourth grade, it is going nowhere. She does not do her homework. The teachers know it. They complain all the time that she daydreams in class and is not focused. When I come home from work, I drop everything and begin the daily struggle to get her to sit and do her homework. It starts with nice words and ends with screaming and punishments. In the end, I find myself dictating to her all the answers and practically doing her homework for her. I'm exhausted and no longer have the strength for these confrontations. I don't know whether what I'm doing is right. Maybe I should give up and leave that task to the teacher."*

When the coach asked what Liora expected from the process, she answered: *"I expect to reach a better understanding of what is happening to Almog, so that I will have the ability to be patient with her and stop arguing with her during our confrontations. I want to comprehend my responsibility as a mother and to what extent I should struggle with her regarding her doing homework. Mostly, I want to restore peace and quiet at home and in my life."*

## To Learn from the Past

The coach should focus on the issue of interventions to date with both the parent and child. Such interventions may be: parental guidance, parents' groups, psychological treatment and the like. Intervention with the child could include: emotional treatment, support groups, various therapies, and the like. It is reasonable to assume that the parent-in-training seeks training after he has experienced a variety of intervention plans. Accordingly, the coach's role is to assist the parent in analyzing and comprehending the reasons as to why such plans have met with success or lack thereof. What part was played by the parent or the child in their success or failure? Developing such insights is imperative for the parent-in-training in order to enable him to observe the course he traversed from the perspective of time, and reach the requisite understanding that will contribute to the success of the forthcoming training process. Gaining such insight is equally important for the coach, so that he will become aware of what has been tried to date and thus learn from past experience.

It is important that the coach should hear the parent-in-training, that he should gather impressions and understand the following:

- **What transpired in that intervention?**
- **What worked and what didn't?**

- **What are the reasons for success/failure?**
- **Of the successes and failures, what may be attributed to the parent and what may be attributed to the child?**

The goal of the dialogue is to enable the parent-in-training to become aware of his share in attaining the results of the previous interventions, and have him differentiate his difficulties from his child's. It is vital that the parent-in-training understand the reasons for his success, partial success and failures, respectively.

## The Big Picture

Most often the coach will be able to see the overall picture before it comes into focus for the parent-in-training, the coach will remain doubtful about it at this juncture and continue to examine his assumptions about it. The coach walks step-by-step with the parent-in-training till the big picture is revealed to the latter and they both actually succeed in perceiving a similar vision.

## Initial Training Target

At the end of the encounter we want to have the parent-in-training focused on the initial training target. We would first review what has happened so far during the encounter: the introduction, elucidating the reasons that brought the parent-in-training into the process, his expectations of this process and ascertaining the interventions to date.

Then, we would ask him: "**Of all that you have described till now, what do you think is the main difficulty – which, if we dealt with, would bring about the turning point?**"

There are parents-in-training who, due to the many difficulties they are facing, might be at a loss as to where to begin. Because they arrive over-saturated, they will find it hard to isolate a single thread from the tapestry of hardships, or alternatively, they might find it difficult to distinguish between the core issue and its various expressions.

We would ask the parent-in-training: "**Of all that you have told us, what is the goal that you would like to achieve as a result of this training process, which would assist you in handling the main challenge you have delineated?**"

We then will write the goal, as it was described by the parent-in-training in his own words, which will serve as raw material for the coach, and which will assist him to shift to a more advanced stage in the process down the road. It is the proverbial tip of the iceberg, and it will be required, during the subsequent encounters, to go deeper and deeper in order to reach the core. The training target will undergo transformation later on, as the coach and parent-in-training further refine it and proceed to crystallize it along the way.

## The Training Contract

The training contract is the start of a covenant, of a relationship in which both sides desire its success. Acceptance of the contract by both the coach and the parent-in-training is actually the expression of assent to committing oneself to a long term relationship. The training relationship is akin to charging a battery, a place where the parent-in-training gets connected to a source of energy, till it will serve to enable him to overcome obstacles in his life. He will not be able to function when his energy level is low, thus charging his batteries is vital. The empowerment does not come directly from the coach, but from the relationship that the two build between themselves.

Within the contract framework, the coach explains to the parent-in-training that he is committing himself to utter sincerity and authenticity in his future interaction with the parent-in-training. In other words, the coach is committing himself to informing the parent-in-training when he disagrees with him or when he feels that the parent-in-training deviates from objective reality.

In order to form a binding dialogue with the parent-in-training, the coach will repeat and emphasize the main tenets written in the contract:

- Training is composed of 13 sessions, 12 encounters (including the first one) and a follow-up six months later.

- The encounters are conducted in person, once a week, in coordination between the coach and the parent-in-training.
- Each encounter will last 90 minutes.
- During the encounters, missions to be performed at home as practice will be provided and their execution is vital for progress in the process.
- The means of communication between the coach and the parent-in-training will be determined.
- The commitment to confidentiality will be emphasized.

## The Mission to Be Performed at Home

We will ask the parent-in-training to document his thoughts, contemplations, frustrations, and insights during the following week. To do that, we will ask him to write a "journey diary" in a notebook that will be especially dedicated for that purpose and accompany him along the training process.

## Summation for the Parent-in-Training

During the final moments of the encounter, the parent-in-training will answer a set of questions, entitled: *Summation Inquiries for the Parent-in-Training*, as follows:[6]

6. See Navigation Sheet No. 2, p. 60.

- **What are your insights as a result of the encounter?**
- **Did anything strike you as particularly significant during the encounter?**
- **Is there any specific question you think I should have asked but didn't?**
- **Is there anything you would have done differently?**
- **Is there anything at all that you'd like to add?**

## First Encounter

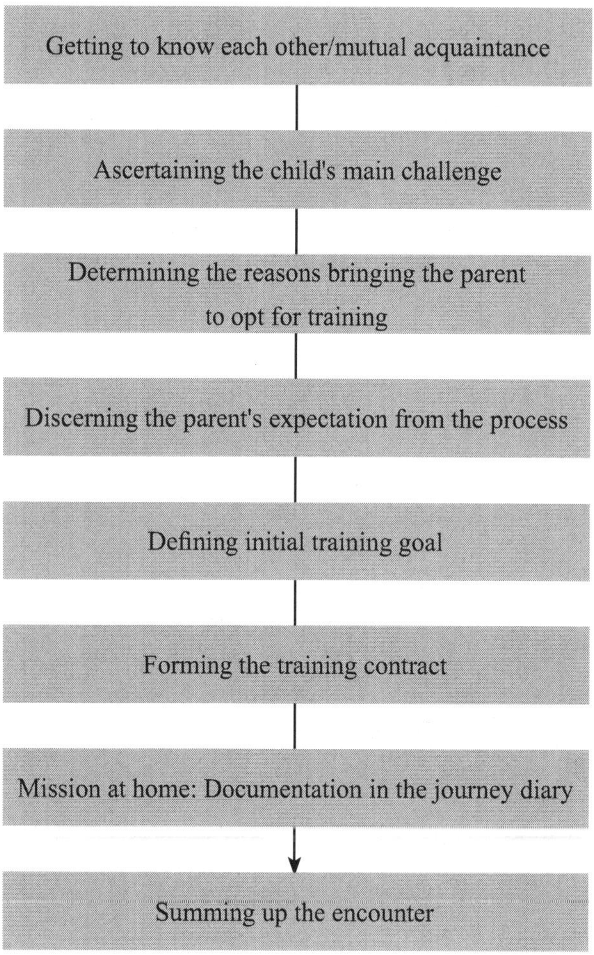

### Navigation Sheet No. 1 for the Coach

## Causes and Expectations

We will ascertain with the parent-in-training the causes that have led him to seek training, and what his expectations are from the process. Thus, we will ask:

What has caused you to seek training?

What are your expectations concerning the training process?

### Navigation Sheet No. 2 for the Coach

## Summary for the Parent-in-Training

We will ask the parent-in-training the following questions during the final few minutes and write down his words.

What are your insights as a result of the encounter?

________________________________________________

________________________________________________

________________________________________________

________________________________________________

________________________________________________

________________________________________________

________________________________________________

________________________________________________

Did anything strike you as particularly significant during the encounter?

________________________________________________

________________________________________________

________________________________________________

________________________________________________

________________________________________________

________________________________________________

________________________________________________

________________________________________________

________________________________________________

Is there any specific question you think I should have asked but didn't?

Is there anything you would have done differently?

Is there anything at all that you'd like to add?

## Second Encounter

# Future Picture

During the first part of the encounter we will encourage the parent-in-training to imagine a future vision of his child. Utilizing this vision, the coach motivates the parent-in-training and takes him away from his daily routine of the 'here and now' to where he could envision his child in a realistic future setting that is anchored in an experience the parent undergoes in the present.

In the second part of the encounter, we will prepare the parent-in-training for an encounter with his child, and practice with him the basics for closeness-enhancing communication.

## Connecting the Encounters

During the first encounter, the parent-in-training has over-saturated the coach with the difficulties and predicaments with which he is struggling. In order to link the first encounter to the one that has followed – and concurrently convey to the parent-in-training the message that he is important to you – it is recommended to ask the parent-in-training about his well-being, find out how his past week was, and inquire whether he wrote anything in his journey diary.

The coach can turn to the parent-in-training and tell him: *"After you left here last week, I pondered what had transpired during the previous encounter. I would like to revisit, in greater depth, the significance of what you said."*

## Departing the "Swamp" for a Bright Future

The parent-in-training is in a "swamp" – a place in which he feels he is sinking in a sea of difficulties, walking in place, not advancing. Departing the "swamp" to a place of optimism and bright outlook toward such a potential future is possible by imagining a future vision, with which he can get on a new path. The parent-in-training will be required to transport himself and his child from the 'here and now' to a future locale where he can succeed in envisioning his child. Such vision creates positive motivation to cope and to depart from where he is wedged, swamped and blocked.

## Future Still Picture

We will ask the parent-in-training: **"How do you envision your child in the future?"**[7] We will ask him to use his imagination to turn the wheels of time and see in his mind's eye a still picture of a future, the farthest in time he can. We will ask him to close his eyes, think for a moment as he is envisioning a future image from a virtual album, in as much detail as he possibly can.

A still picture is immobile, freezing at a point in time of a given event or experience. Our picture albums are stuffed full of stills from various times in our lives, representing the important things and persons in our existence. Generating a future still picture in the parent-in-training's imagination is a powerful tool that enables him to tangibly visualize his child in the future: where he will be, those around him, the colors, the scents and feelings accompanying it all. The picture represents the manner by which the parent-in-training can see his child disengaged from the 'here and now' and allows him to get in tune with what is truly significant. The temporal dimension may differ from one parent to another. Some parents-in-training are able to imagine their child's high school graduation, while others can only see their child a few months hence, e.g., at the start of the following year. The coach does not get involved in determining the moment in time and

7. See Navigation Sheet No. 3, p. 93.

allows the parent to choose, for this dimension is indicative of the parent's specific struggle, the one that makes it hard for him to disengage from the 'here and now.'

As a metaphor for taking a still picture with a camera, the coach will ask the parent-in-training to help the former see the picture clearly, to zoom in on the details. Now the parent will be asked to describe it in minute detail. Here are a few sample questions to hone in on the depiction:

- **Where do you see your child? Where is he?**
- **How does he look?**
- **What exactly is he doing there?**
- **What is he wearing?**
- **What is occupying him?**
- **Who is he with?**
- **Who are his friends?**
- **How does he feel? Is he happy? Is he glad? Sad? Concerned? Relaxed?**
- **Does he demonstrate self-confidence?**

At times the parent-in-training does not settle for a single still picture but also tells a story. It is the coach's role to depict a specific picture – not tell a story.

## Possible Scenarios

Experience teaches us that there are three probable scenarios:

1. The parent-in-training is able to see a bright, optimistic future vision of his child.
2. The parent-in-training is able to see his child in the future; however, the picture is a pessimistic one.
3. The parent-in-training is unable to see a future picture of his child.

## First Scenario: Optimistic Picture

This is the most common scenario. It is reasonable to assume that most of the parents-in-training will be able to see an optimistic future picture of their child and describe it to the coach, as it appears in his or her imagination.

## Real & Unrealistic Picture

Ask the parent: "**What you are envisioning, what particular moment do you choose to freeze in the frame?**"
"**Is the picture you envision based on the reality you are experiencing today?**"
The parent-in-training relating to a realistic picture, one that is based on his familiarity with his child in the present, will be able to project from the

child's areas of current strength, areas where he is successful, talented and has been positively noticed, even acknowledged.
The difference between a realistic and unrealistic vision (the parental fantasy) is significant at this juncture, since the parent's fantasy is an expression of denial and represents a fanciful notion of the parent, stemming from his refusal to acknowledge the loss of the perfect child.

## Ron's Graduation

Alona sought training because of her 10-year-old son, Ron. In her vision she described Ron as an 18-year-old adolescent at his high school graduation ceremony. He stands confidently on stage and plays a major role in a theatrical production. He is elated, but not agitated, and everybody applauds him. For her, the momentous event is that it is all occurring so naturally for Ron in that future event. *"He is so much at ease, in harmony with it."* She expressed an apprehension about not being able to determine whether it was her or his dream. She said: *"Is it realistic at all? Maybe he won't even make it to the 12th Grade."* Then she proceeded to say: *"If it will be fulfilled, for me it will unload a great burden. We shall have done it and then we'll be able to rest."*

## Ruthie, Store Manager

Anat sought training because of her 15-year-old daughter, Ruthie. She described her vision: *"Ruthie is managing a very big computer store and is in charge of a large staff. She is the kind of person who is able to not only provide technical solutions, but also solve human relation problems... she is able to tune into the customer and his desires, and, most significantly – endow people around her with positive feelings. She is not the kind of person who get bogged down in minutiae ... she sees a problem and says: 'Let's solve it and go on from there...' She has fabulous management skills. I see her in a representative outfit with a lot of grace and a smile. It seems that she is well, that she is utilizing her ability and that she exudes satisfaction."*

## Grace, Joyous & Happy

Irit arrived for training due to her 13-year-old daughter, Grace. She is an avid sports enthusiast, swimming in particular. In her future vision, Irit saw Grace participating in a swim meet, *"not as a member of a nationally ranking club, but in a team that formed in a community. She stands at the pool, her golden wavy hair flowing down her shoulders; she is ready and focused on the mission ahead. She takes third place and is awarded a medal. Everybody comes to greet and congratulate her, to hug her and cheer. She is in the center, surrounded; she is joyous and happy."*

## Second Scenario: Pessimistic Picture

In this scenario the parent-in-training is able to form a future vision; however, it is a pessimistic one. In this case, he pours out his fears, his feelings of hardship and anguish, which obscure reality and prevent him from seeing the positive aspects his child is endowed with. He has so much despair that he paints his child's future in dark and bleak colors.

## Hard, Painful Moment

Describing a pessimistic picture is a very hard and painful moment for the parent-in-training. This may be the first time he admits it or shares it with another. Consequently, in such a difficult moment he will need appreciation and emotional reinforcement from the coach, for the sheer effort and the courage he summoned in order to communicate the gloomy vision he just had.

As coaches, we do not flinch when we find ourselves at this cheerless moment, thus we allow the parent-in-training to be there. We consider both the optimistic and pessimistic manifestations as springboards of equal utility for our work with the parent-in-training. Each holds within it 'raw materials' the coach will need in his work.

## The Role of the Coach

At this charged moment we will carefully avoid giving advice and offering solutions – even when it clearly appears that such would be the salvation of the parent-in-training or would bestow a sense of well-being on him – that he received a practical solution during the training process.

It is crucial that solutions and advice spring from the parent-in-training himself, for he has all the answers within himself. Only ideas that originate from him will create the difference between all the advice he has received to date and the process he is immersed in now.

## Pessimistic Picture:

### First Option for Action

The role of the coach is to assist the parent-in-training to try and see a positive spark, one that will transform the harsh reality he has just experienced. We will ask him to clarify, so that we can ascertain what precisely he has envisioned in order to try and transform the discouraging reality of the vision. We will ask clarifying questions, so we can determine all that he saw, to enable us to unearth a positive outlook, which we will draw attention to.

We will ask: **Is there anything you could alter in the picture? If so, please describe what you see now.**

After having been presented with these inquiries, occasionally the parent-in-training will present an alternative vision. We will examine what has changed and where exactly the shift has occurred. We will ask: **"What did you alter in the picture? How does it differ from what you've seen previously?"**

## Pessimistic Picture:

### Second Option for Action

In case the parent-in-training is unable to alter the pessimistic vision, assistance may be provided with guiding questions, such as:

- **What was the first thought/feeling that came to mind when you pondered the vision?**
- **If you could, which element would you remove and which would you retain in the picture?**
- **What is the least threatening/frightening aspect in the depiction?**
- **What are the picture's colors?**

## A Video

When the picture is really hard to take, it will be equally hard for the parent-in-training to modify it. In such a case, we suggest to expand the viewing angle and convert the still picture into a video. In this manner we enable the coach and the parent-in-training to better understand what is transpiring and its causes.

Sample Questions:

- **What happened just before snapping the still picture?**
- **What happened just after snapping the still picture?**
- **How did your child arrive at that particular place?**
- **Who took the picture?**
- **What would your child do next? Where will he go from here?**

If the picture remains pessimistic, we will check with the parent-in-training as to what he could do today in order to avoid the gloomy prediction of the picture in his depiction. The parent may discuss a single, minor detail – one that may be altered. We will ask: "**Let's think together: What can be done differently today to avoid having the picture become manifest in reality? What can you, the parent, do in order to craft a change in the circumstances?**"

Our task as coaches is to cause the parent-in-training to reflect on and undermine the vision. Any variation, as minute as it might be, could lead to additional positive changes.

## A Bright Spark in a Bleak Picture

Just as the coach had made the request for a description of a future still picture of Tal, Irit said that it was very hard for her: a desolate, negative picture arose. When the coach asked for its description, Irit said: *"Tal is 13. He sits alone in his room, alone at the computer, watching dumb wrestling stuff. Heavy metal is playing in the background. The colors of the picture are dark: black and brown."*

When the coach asked her what was so difficult for her in the picture, she answered: *"I know that there is a long and complicated road ahead of me, one that's complex and endless. All the 'normal' things that mothers anticipate their sons to accomplish – I do not expect from Tal. I do not know whether he will graduate, I do not know whether he will serve in the army, I'm not sure he will have a family of his own. I do not expect anything from him anymore."*

In response to the coach's inquiry of what should happen for all these predictions to be reversed, she answered: *"He must awaken from the inner world he's trapped in. He needs to open up to the world outside and people in close proximity to him."*

The coach then asked Irit, in what situation does she think Tal would be able to open up to those around him, to which she replied: *"When he feels good about himself, with a positive self-image."*

When the coach asked if there was specific datum she would have changed in her vision, she said: *"I would have changed the computer games he's playing.*

*Maybe instead of wrestling he could play trivia or some other such game. All this nonsense on the computer is nothing but a waste of time. If he could use this tool to develop his mind, then there will be a spark for an alternative future picture where he possibly could even succeed in the field of computers, maybe high-tech, and make a career of it."*

## Third Scenario: Parent Unable to See a Future Picture of His Child

In this scenario the parent-in-training is unable to see a picture of his child's future at all. A parent who is unable to see any picture whatsoever is in a more difficult place than the parent who saw a pessimistic picture, for he avoids giving voice to his fears and apprehensions. He is unable to cope with his forthcoming challenges, thus he opts for avoidance. He has trouble seeing the picture because he is immersed in a "swamp" and is preoccupied with his daily survival. In such a case, we will find out why it is too demanding for him to envision his child's future picture. With guiding questions we will assist the parent to extract some sort of a picture that he can see. It may be a vision of only a very near future, but it would still allow the parent to develop a perspective (distance) from where he is. This way would ease his difficulty in understanding the reality he is enmeshed in and consider other and new courses for coping.

We will tell the parent-in-training that by lifting a

magic wand, with a wave of a hand, we have done away with all his child's tribulations. We then will ask the parent-in-training: **"Describe your child without his difficulties."** We will request that the parent close his eyes and describe a picture of his child. The idea is to disengage him from the 'here and now' and have him find himself in an alternative time frame, one that's more optimistic. We will examine what the parent-in-training sees now in his future vision, after we have 'removed' the obstacles to its formation. The picture should ignite the parent-in-training's transport to an optimistic mindset, where he will notice certain positive aspects previously invisible to him.

## Dalia's Fear

When the coach asked Dalia to describe her daughter Danna's future still picture, she said: *"It is very hard for me to see her in the future, even the near one. I can't, I'm not able. It's even hard for me to think about it."*

The coach sought to bring her to see it in a very close proximity, in order to further develop the vision from that point. Dalia responded, *"I simply cannot do it."* When asked what frightens her so much, she answered: *"Those around her, the kind of company she keeps."*

In order to help Dalia, the coach resorted to magic – which made those specific difficulties instantly vanish – then asked her to describe her daughter's future picture after the deletion. Dalia spoke haltingly: *"Dana is in (army) uniform ... unkempt hair..."*

## Progressing Toward the Goal

When the future vision is clear and realistic, it is the time to examine, together with the parent-in-training, how to convert the vision into a reality in the future.
We will ask the parent-in-training: **"What are you doing today in order to further your child to the place you have described?"**
We will check with the parent to determine what advances him toward the goal and what hinders him.

## Drawing the Training Zone

The picture allows us to draw the *Training Zone*, which is an expanse where the coach and the parent-in-training operate. Later on, it will let us define the training goal and hone it into clarity. The parent-in-training enters the process completely full of conflicts with his child: Difficulties in learning, in getting organized, social difficulties and more. Of all the challenges he is enumerating, we want to know which one is the most important to him. It may be that he will seek approval for the manner with which he deals with his child, to restore his parental authority or the connection he has lost with his child. That would define the training zone for us.

The parent will not be able to make it from the training zone to the training goal without our assistance and support. Thus, we would divide the path into sections, lower a ladder and assist him to ascend step by step toward the training goal. The goal centers him on the obstacles he has to overcome – but also on the opportunities embedded in such a process. In this course, the parent will be able to look back and see the road he has traveled already that led him to the training goal.

## Future Vision as Raw Material

In every future picture that has been described by the parent-in-training, a range of contents and emotions comes to the surface. It will not always be possible for the coach to relate to all of them in this encounter. This 'raw material' will be utilized by the coach down the road. He will be able to use it to demonstrate and employ the contents that have surfaced to draw therefrom, new insights and understandings throughout the training process.

## The Difficulty from the Child's Viewpoint

We will ask the parent in-training what, in his mind, the child thinks about his difficulty; what does the child consider to be a difficulty?

- **How, do you think, your child would describe his difficulty?**

- **How does it express itself?**
- **What is it that bothers him the most?**
- **Would he describe the difficulty as that of those around him (parents/school/others) or as his own?**

The purpose of the questions is to refine the parent's listening ability, so that he can hear the subtle nuances between what he thinks and knows about his child and what his child feels and thinks.
At the next step we will seek to hear from the child.

## The Mission to Be Performed at Home

We will ask the parent-in-training to set an appointment with his child, whose purpose is to understand the child's challenges from his point of view. We will explain to him that the meeting should take place in comfortable and pleasant surroundings for both, at a time which they will mutually agree upon. At times, it will be desirable that the meeting takes place outside their residence – at a café or a restaurant, on the beach, or at any place the child suggests – because "it will be fun there."

## A Meeting of the Parent-in-Training with His Child

Listening to the child is a crucial key for a true dialogue, one that enables growth and development of the parent-in-training and his child. Such dialogue is feasible when the parent-in-training's ability to hear details is sharpened and refined, and when he conveys to his child that he understands him and his emotional state. Often, the child has already ceased sharing his feelings with others, after tiring from the many efforts he made to make them known. In order to encourage him to open up, the parent-in-training could improve his capacity for forming empowering discourse with his child, one that allows an honest expression of the struggles experienced by the child. As the parent discovers the art of listening, the child realizes that his voice is heard and that someone really cares for him. In turn, from the example supplied by the parent-in-training he develops listening skills of his own.

Because observation and imitation of others is a main human learning method, observing those who present adaptive behavior ought to teach individuals lacking good adaptive responses better coping strategies. Thus, the trainee observes the coach and the child observes the parent. Consequently, learning takes place.

## Parallel Processes

The processes occurring between the parent-in-training and the coach transpire concurrently with those taking place between the parent and his child. In every encounter, the dialogue between the coach and the parent-in-training serve as an imitation model for the discourse between parent and child. The parent-in-training experiences listening, empathy and being understood without judgment and criticism, thus he feels that he has arrived at a place where he is included and understood. Such empowering experience enables learning. When the coach provides him access to this very special place, he actually teaches the parent, indirectly, implicitly, how to interact with his child. From this place, the parent-in-training and his child may conduct a deep, meaningful exchange from within, which will form a subtle and profound connection between them.

Through such an approach communication and the ability to ask the child open-ended and engaging questions, understanding of the child and his real needs may be had, as well as identification with his struggles and the commitment to stand by him. The key is where the parent-in-training will succeed in genuinely listening to his child and understanding his difficulties – as he experiences them – for no one else will be able to authentically describe them.

## Pentecost[8] Ceremony

Orna arrived for training in order to receive means that would assist her to cope with her child's disability. She did not always understand why he refused

8. A prominent feast in the Jewish calendar celebrating the giving of the Torah at Sinai (later entering the Christian liturgical year, commemorating the descent of the Holy Spirit upon the disciples).

to cooperate in school activities, mostly when it came to parties and ceremonies. She divulged that the teacher summoned her and said: *"It's a pity that Yaron does not participate in the Shavuot (Pentecost) ceremony,"* while she had no idea that he declined participation; he did not tell her a thing about the matter.

In a subsequent discussion with her son, Yaron, he told her: *"It's a dumb and stupid ceremony and who needs it anyhow?"* Orna responded: *"There are thirty children in your class, some no less intelligent than you, and if they can participate so can you."* When an argument ensued about the subject, he burst out crying and said: *"I'll never be able to figure out how to perform the dance they did at the ceremony."* On the day of the ceremony Yaron went up to his mother and during the dance he told her: *"I don't understand why I am not participating – I know the steps as well as they do."* Orna explained to him that now he knows that prior to the ceremony, rehearsals are held and the dance is practiced; that next time he, too, will be able to take part.

He replied: *"Mom, you understand nothing. If I had participated in the rehearsals I wouldn't have learned a thing. I know how to do it, because I've watched them during the rehearsals."*

Thus Orna learned that since Yaron had difficulty in planning movement, he got confused and that had worked to devastate his social standing, which led him to avoid participating in the ceremony. Through the dialogue with his mother, Yaron dis-

covered that such a ceremony was not intimidating and Orna gained knowledge about her son's particular difficulties through his perspective.
This kind of dialogue will assist her in the future, as additional manifestations of this nature appear. After having that dialogue Orna said: *"I have learned that in order to understand Yaron I have to see things through his eyes. The key to success is discussing the learning disability with your child."*

## Preparations for Parent-Child Dialogue:

### Experience in Closeness-Enhancing Communication

Since one of the main goals of training is to create a communication channel between parent and child, practicing a closeness-enhancing communication approach – as a continuous process all through training – will, no doubt, assist the parent-in-training in maximizing his objective knowledge of the difficulty entailed in his child's struggle, and the implications of such difficulties on his life and his emotional well-being. In order to assist the parent to understand his child's point of view, we will offer a role-playing simulation, where the parent-in-training plays his child and the coach steps into the parent's shoes. Such simulation allows the parent to try and understand what goes through his child's mind regarding his challenges, what he considers a difficulty, what he is struggling with and the range of emotions that accompany all that. This way, the parent-in-training gets to have a learning experience that facilitates the actual experience of feelings and adverse circumstances his child goes through. Also, he gets to experience "as a child" the interaction with the coach, who assumes the role of the parent temporarily. The manner in which questions by the coach – as the parent-in-training – come across, in effect prepares the parent for the encounter with his child. In this practice, the parent will be trained how to utilize closeness-enhancing communication.

## Guidelines for the Conversation

We will explain to the parent-in-training that the purpose of the conversation is a dialogue – not a monologue – with his child. We will make it clear to him that he doesn't need to take responsibility for the discourse and its course, but to talk from a place that allows listening, holding, empathy and understanding, while using closeness-enhancing communications.

## Closeness-Enhancing Communication

In closeness-enhancing communication an emphasis is placed on saying "I" and that in this conversation there is no place for interpretations, criticism or judgment.

It is an encounter that facilitates mutually free expression of feelings and emotions, an expression that paves the way to a dialogue that contains sharing, intimacy and free flow of interaction. Such communication highlights what the parties have in common and the ability to overcome conflicts, disagreements, controversies and differences in positions.

## Samples of Closeness-Enhancing Communication

I feel that …

I think that …

In my opinion …

I find it important …

It has awakened in me … Did you feel the same? …

It stirred me …

I am saddened to hear ….

I find it hard to …

I am willing to reconsider ….

## Taking the Conversation to a Deeper Level

The coach will instruct the parent-in-training that his questions should be short and the child's answer ought to be long. Moreover, when the child speaks the parent-in-training should seek to expand the conversation, take it deeper, with such questions as:

- What do you mean?
- How did you feel? What did you think?
- What does it resemble?
- What would you have happen differently? What does that depend on?
- Did I understand/hear you correctly when you said…?

The goal is to build a deep as well as wide conversation, to avoid a 'Ping-Pong' type discussion; instead, it should be a discourse replete with pondering, attentiveness, empathy and getting a feel for the child, letting him know that his accounts are interesting, fascinating and exciting to the parent-in-training.

It is important to clarify to the parent-in-training that such a discussion is not easy to accomplish, and therefore requires meticulous preparation and prior practice. Often, during the initial exercise, the parent feels a great deal of embarrassment and even finds it hard to come up with words to say. It is crucial that the difficulty and embarrassment come up in the training session rather than during the conversation with his child.

It is highly recommended to practice by role-playing where the parent plays his child as the coach plays the parent.

## The Role of the Coach

During the role-playing exercise, it is the coach's job to provide feedback regarding the communication manner utilized and point out where the parent-in-training strayed from the dialogue of closeness-enhancing communication. We have to guide him how to word his expressions, while praising his readiness to attempt to carry them out. We will recommend to the parent-in-training to write down in his journey diary examples and sentences that could assist him during the meeting with his child.

## Insights

For the parent-in-training to internalize the sense of attentiveness, holding and letting go of criticism and judgment, it is recommended that at the end of the encounter we will ask him: **"What are your understandings now as a result of the training you've received today, the ones you will arrive with at the meeting with your child? What did you feel when we talked?**

## The Mission to Be Performed at Home

## Commencing the Conversation

In order to 'break the ice' and harness the child's cooperation, we would advocate commencing the conversation by discussing the child's strengths and abilities, and only then proceed to deal with his difficulties. One may start with the same question the parent-in-training was just asked: **"How do you see yourself in the future?"** We suggest that the parent-in-training ask his child-guiding questions, such as:

- Where are you?
- How do you look? What are you wearing?
- What are you doing there?
- What keeps you busy?
- Who do you hang around with?
- Tell me about your buddies.
- How do you feel? Are you happy? Are you sad? Anxious? Relaxed?
- Do you feel confident?

## Openness and Cooperation

As the conversation ensues, we would recommend to the parent-in-training to bring his child openly and clearly into the training process in which he is taking part, share his thoughts and feelings with his child, the difficulties he is undergoing and his great desire to support his child without making mistakes, as well as his wish to acquire tools and strength.

For example:

*"Lately, I think about you a lot and, actually, I fail to fully comprehend your difficulties and how you'd have*

*it differently. I have a feeling that we're racing, trying to find solutions during our daily routines, but we do not take the time, as we are engaged in all our chores and tasks, to do it properly. I want to stop and to gain insight into your struggle. Give me an example of something that's hard for you. I truly wish to be of help to you and do all that's in my power to make you feel content. "I'm going through a training process where I was asked, 'what is your main challenge'? I thought that your main challenge is ________. I wanted to clarify it with you: Do you, too, feel that's your main challenge? Do you see it that way, also?"*

## The Conversation's Conclusion

We would advise the parent-in-training to end the conversation with a positive, jovial statement, such as: *"I've had a very special day with you today ... it was so much fun to have spent it with you ... "* Ending on a positive note, reinforcing and stressing the positive quality of the experience, will encourage the child to return to such conversations in the future.

## Summing up the Encounter with the Child

We will ask the parent-in-training, right after the meeting with his child, to answer the following question:[9]

9. See Navigation Sheet No. 4, p. 95.

## Formal Aspects

- Where did you get together?
- How did your child respond to the invitation for a meeting?
- Whose idea was it where to meet?
- How long did it last?

## Content of the Dialogue

- What was discussed at the meeting?
- Did your child cooperate?
- How much did you talk and how much did your child talk?
- Did the conversation flow unhindered? Or were there blocks or an impedance during the conversation? If so, why did they materialize? How did you cope with them as a parent? How did your child respond?

## Fulfillment of Expectations

- What were your expectations of the encounter just prior to its occurrence? Did they materialize?
- How did the meeting with your child contribute to your understanding of his struggles and challenges?
- How does your child see himself in the future?

## Summation for the Parent-in-Training

During the final moments of the encounter, the parent-in-training will answer a set of questions, entitled: *Summation Inquiries for the Parent-in-Training*, as follows:[10]

- **What are your insights as a result of the encounter?**
- **Did anything strike you as particularly significant during the encounter?**
- **Is there any specific question you think I should have asked but didn't?**
- **Is there anything you would have done differently?**
- **Is there anything at all that you'd like to add?**

10. See Navigation Sheet No. 2, p. 99.

## The Second Encounter

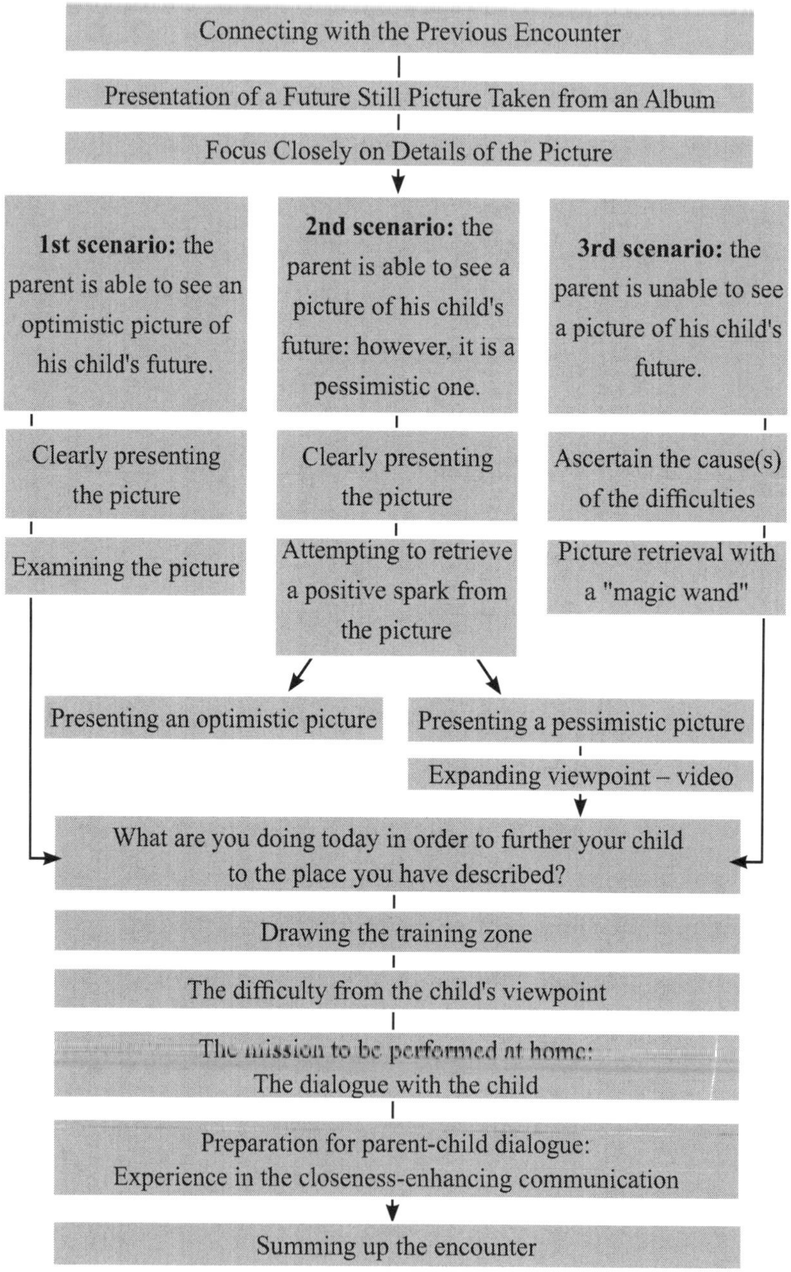

### Navigation Sheet No. 3 for the Coach

## Future Still Picture

We will ask the parent-in-training: "**How do you envision your child in the future?**" We will ask him to use his imagination, to turn the wheels of time and see in his mind's eye a still picture of a future, the farthest in time he can. We will ask him to close his eyes, think for a quick moment as he is envisioning a future image from a virtual album, describing it in as much detail as he possibly can.

We will guide the parent to describe a picture, not tell a story.

We will write his description word for word.

For example: *"I see my daughter sitting in the living room with friends. They are watching a movie and she is snuggled up in a blanket ..."*

### Navigation Sheet No. 4 for the Parent-in-Training

## Questions to the Parent-in-Training Following the Encounter with His Child

Please answer the following questions:

### Formal Aspects

Where did you get together?

How did your child respond to the invitation for a meeting?

Whose idea was it where to meet?

How long did it last?

## Dialogue's Content

What was discussed at the meeting?

Did your child cooperate?

How much did you talk and how much did your child talk?

Did the conversation flow unhindered, or were there blocks or inhibitions during the conversation? If so, why did they materialize? How did you cope with them as a parent? How did the child respond?

## Fulfillment of Expectations

What were your expectations of the encounter just prior to its occurrence? Did they materialize?

How did the meeting with your child contribute to your understanding of his struggles and challenges?

How does your child see himself in the future?

### Navigation Sheet No. 2 for the Coach

## Summation for the Parent-in-Training

During the final moments of the encounter, the parent-in-training will answer a set of questions; we will write down his words:

What are your insights as a result of the encounter?

Did anything strike you as particularly significant during the encounter?

Is there any specific question you think I should have asked but didn't?

Is there anything you would have done differently?

Is there anything at all that you'd like to add?

## Third Encounter

# Dialogue With the Child

During this encounter the parent-in-training defines the first training goal following the dialogue he had held with his child. The coach will assist him to choose a modest and attainable objective that will allow him to experience progress and success.

### Connection Between Encounters

During the first two encounters we dealt with the training goal while putting the emphasis on the parent-in-training's point of view. The current encounter is taking place after the parent has held a dialogue with his child. Therefore, this is an opportune occasion to allow us to incorporate the child's viewpoint, in redefining and refining the initial training goal.

Initially, we ask the parent as to his well-being. We will inquire as to the past week's events and we will discuss his meeting with his child, which should have occurred already.

## Possible Scenarios

Our experience instructs us that there are two probable scenarios:

1. The parent-in-training met his child.
2. The parent-in-training did not meet his child.

## First Scenario:
## The Parent-in-Training Met With His Child

There are parents who come back thrilled and excited from the meeting with their child. They feel that it has exposed them to many previously unknown regions: *"It was such an exciting encounter, I'll never forget it. It was a magical evening. I've learned that he desires more independence in making his choices."*

## Parent-Child Dialogue

Through the contents described by the parent the child will 'appear', thus we get to meet him.
We will use our home mission, the one provided at the second encounter, and ask:

## Formal Aspects

- Where did you get together?
- How did your child respond to the invitation for a meeting?
- Whose idea was it where to meet?
- What was discussed at the meeting?
- How long did it last?

## Content of the Dialogue

- What was said during the meeting?
- Did your child cooperate?
- How much did you talk and how much did your child talk?
- Did the conversation flow unhindered? Or were there blocks or an impedance during the conversation? If so, why did they materialize? How did you cope with them as a parent? How did the child respond?

## Fulfillment of Expectations

- What were your expectations of the encounter just prior to its occurrence? Did they materialize?

- How did the meeting with your child contribute to your understanding of his struggles and challenges?
- How does your child see himself in the future?

## A Different Kind of Dialogue

In order to ascertain whether a different kind of dialogue took place between child and parent, the coach will ask the parent:

**Is there anything new you've learned about your child as a result of the conversation with him?**

If the parent answers that indeed he has learned something new about his child, we could assume that a dialogue did take place between them.

However, if the parent claims that he had learned nothing new, we can conclude that either no dialogue took place or that the parent is unaware of what had transpired and is unable to ascertain what he had learned about his child from the dialogue.

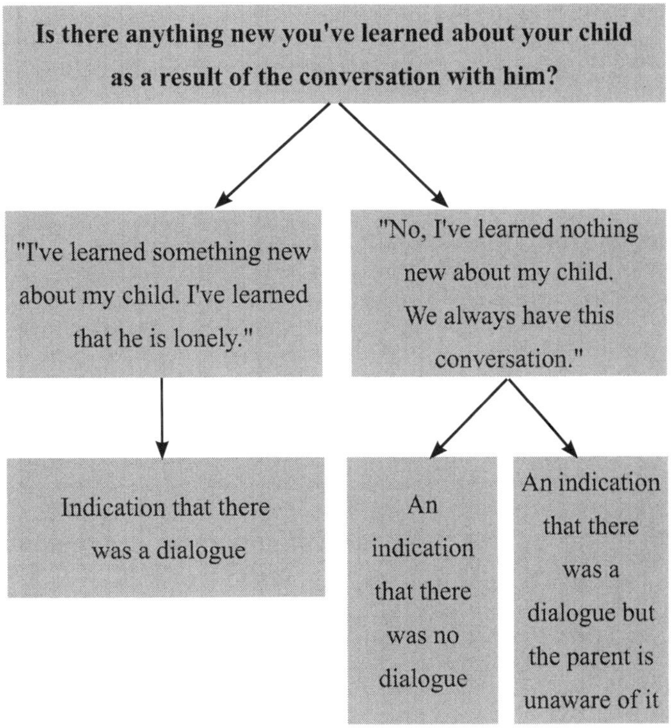


When we are engaged with a different kind of a dialogue, the parent trains to listen to his child and learns something new. Such dialogue is devoid of judgment and criticism. It is a new type of dialogue between them that rises to a new level from the previous one they held.

At times, the parent-in-training needs the coach's assistance, using investigative questions in order to ascertain that, in fact, a dialogue did take place where he had learned something new of which he was unaware previously.

## Second Scenario:
## The Parent-in-Training Did Not Meet With His Child

There could be several reasons accounting for the fact that no encounter had occurred between the parent and child: Some may be technical in nature, others stemming from the parent's apprehensions, which have caused delay and avoidance of the meeting.

*"We've had a very busy week, and could not find the time." Or, "I don't understand why a special meeting should take place; I talk to him at home all the time."*

It is the coach's role to relate to the reasons leading to the failure. The coach will not 'admonish' the parent for his not completing the home mission. Instead, he will determine the difficulty encountered and will demonstrate trust and empathy, with neither opinion nor censure, in order to assist him to determine his share in the failure to hold the meeting.

Ask the parent:

- **Why didn't it take place?**
- **Why is it hard for you to meet with your child?**
- **What should occur in order for the meeting to take place?**

## Role Playing

We should re-emphasize the importance of the dialogue between parent and child. This plays an important role in putting the process into motion, where he listens to his child, thus securing better insight into what the child is struggling with. To demonstrate to the parent-in-training the difference between a typical dialogue and the distinctive kind – the one he is asked to participate in at present – we will perform another role-playing game, where he will play the part of the child, who discusses and describes his struggles, while the coach will play the role of the parent.

We will examine it together: Was it a dialogue or just a monologue? We will reiterate that it is important to ascertain whether the parent talked more than his child. In a monologue-type discourse, the parent utters well-worn phrases, to be distinguished from a dialogue, where two participate and exchange ideas.

We will ask the parent-in-training to go back and hold the dialogue with his child, and explain to the parent that the key to the success of the process is attentiveness and listening to the child. Accordingly, it is not feasible to skip the dialogue, without which there will be no progress in the process.

## The Child's Future Picture

We will ask the parent-in-training to describe in words the future vision, as he did during the previous encounter. Then we will ask him to tell us about the future picture evoked by the child at the meeting between them. We will ask him:

**"Is there any difference between the pictures? If so, then what is it?"**

We will try to comprehend the meaning of the difference from the parent's point of view.

## The Child's Difficulty

After we have asked the parent to describe in words his child's difficulty, as he described it during the previous encounter – before meeting his child, we will compare the description of the child and that of the parent in describing the child's struggles: What did the child say and what were the words he used as he described the challenge he is trying to cope with? Equally, we will ascertain what the parent said, and what words he used in portraying the difficulty of his child.

We then will note the differences between the two descriptions, and seek to understand the meaning of the difference from the viewpoint of the parent:

**"What did you consider to be the difficulty in your child's life before the meeting with him?"**

**"What have you learned from the encounter with your child of which you were not aware till now?"**

## The Conversation With Noa

Avi's dialogue with his daughter, Noa, took place one evening prior to his subsequent meeting with the coach. Avi was the one who initiated the conversation. He told Noa that he had homework and asked her if she would be willing to assist him. She was surprised and was genuinely glad to lend him a hand. They decided to have a meeting at the neighborhood café. On their way over there, Avi shared with Noa recent events occurring at his place of work. *"I didn't want her to feel that I was coming to debrief her. I wanted her to feel that it was an opportunity for a cozy conversation in which we both shared our experiences. It lasted an hour and a half, and it was a very pleasant open discussion, not the tense and burdensome event I was dreading. We laughed a lot. There was an amiable ambiance that aided me in asking Noa questions I do not usually ask. I asked her about her social struggles. The year before she was socially isolated, and I needed to know where things stood now. I was surprised to find out she had girlfriends, even some good friends – when she was at home I didn't notice any social activity. I've learned that, contrary to my impression, she did not feel isolated. She talked especially about two really good girlfriends and about a lot of virtual friends on the Internet. We also talked about her learning disabilities. In a very mature way she said that she thinks that the disabilities have both advantages and disadvantages. She even added:* 'I know that I'm not too good with algebraic formulae and in some oth-

ers areas, but I notice what happens around me and I am more involved; and, just because I have some disabilities does not mean I will not be successful in life. Aren't there individuals who were not such great students, yet are rather successful now?'
*"We concluded the conversation by me hugging and kissing her. I thanked her for sharing with me and told her we should do that more often. She said that she, too, enjoyed it immensely."*

## The Parental Authority

Dana arrived to training in order to reinforce her parental authority. She felt that it was loosening up vis-à-vis her 15-year-old son and claimed she was having a hard time disciplining him and maintaining firm guidelines, so as to get him to listen to her. In the dialogue with her son she discovered that, in addition to the daily challenges he was facing, the child expressed additional difficulties. Dana was sure that her son did not experience social disadvantages, that he was always surrounded by friends. However, during their dialogue she learned about his loneliness – that even though he had friends, he felt lonely. *"I do have lots of friends, but not really ... I spend time with them, but I'm actually alone."*
It is this intimate get-together, where Dana met with her son, and through him with his lonesomeness, that enabled both to arrive at a different kind of dialogue, making it meaningful in his eyes. Consequently, he demonstrated greater acceptance of

the guidelines she sets out of her love and concern for him.

## Return to the Training Goal

We will revisit the training goal, as it was characterized by the parent-in-training and we will now examine to what extent, if at all, the characterization has changed following the encounter with the child. We will formulate it from the parent's viewpoint as well as the child's, centering on the latter's difficulties.

## Honing In

At this stage of the training process the training goal is, as a rule, still defined in terms that are too broad and general. By honing in on the dialogue between parent and child, we can isolate – out of the general goal as it was phrased till now – a simple and attainable objective that will allow the parent-in-training to experience progress and success. The coach will ask the parent to describe the simplest objective, one which he considers capable of promoting attainment of the larger goal – something he believes he could accomplish successfully.
This simple objective will provide the parent-in-training with the fuel needed to set himself in pursuit of his new course, while energizing his action as he aims toward an optimal direction.

The idea is to move onto attainable and measurable definitions and present him with a task he can assume, one which allows him to operate with a sense of having the requisite aptitude and capability.

In order for us to arrive at the preferred objective with the parent-in-training, we may say to him:

**You are depicting a large, broad canvas, on which is _____ (for instance, a shift in the relationship with the child/bringing the child into the bosom of the family, etc.). Is there anything you could do on the way to materializing such goal? What do you think you could do this week as you proceed along this path?**

The idea is to formulate a workable task that the parent could undertake and execute.

For example, a parent, whose training goal is to have his child acquire social skills, could set, at the end of the meeting, a specific objective: to help his child be less embarrassed about attending a party his classmates are holding during that particular week.

## First Step on the Path to Transformation

This chosen objective is not the ultimate end of the training, however, it would enable the parent-in-training, already during the next encounter, to examine his performance and take the next step toward refining the outline of the training goal.

At the end of the encounter the coach will examine,

together with the parent-in-training, the chosen objective by way of the following questions:[11]

- **Why, in your role as a parent, is the chosen objective important to you?**
- **Why is the chosen objective important to your child?**
- **What do you expect would occur when you reach the objective?**

## The Mission to Be Performed at Home

Within the home mission framework, the parent is required to advance toward the chosen objective, get underway and perform the task he has outlined. The parent-in-training will document the process and answer the following questions:[12]

- **What action did you take in order to meet the objective?**
- **What was the outcome?**
- **In what way do you think you have progressed toward fulfillment of the training goal?**

---

11. See Navigation Sheet No. 5, p. 117.

12. See Navigation Sheet No. 6, p. 119.

## A Goal with External Focus of Control

Even when a parent-in-training has chosen a concrete objective, which is well-defined and attainable, it does not mean that he would know how to achieve it. During this encounter, the training goal is still perceived as one that is controlled externally. When the focus is on external control, the parent-in-training would tend to consider his external environment as the cause of consequences in his experience, thus avoiding personal responsibility for such consequences. During the next encounter we will therefore focus on the training goal, and refocus its terminology into the zone of internal control, where the parent-in-training will learn to feel responsible for his actions and its consequences and where he will acquire the insight that he has the ability to alter reality.

## Summation for Parents-in-Training

During the last few minutes of the encounter the parent-in-training will answer *Summation Questions for the Parent-in-Training*:[13]

- **What are your insights as a result of the encounter?**
- **Did anything strike you as particularly significant during the encounter?**

---

13. See Navigation Sheet No. 2, p. 121.

- **Is there any specific question you think I should have asked but didn't?**
- **Is there anything you would have done differently?**
- **Is there anything at all that you'd like to add?**

## Feedback

At the conclusion of this encounter, the coach will examine his interaction with the parent-in-training and how the latter feels at the training space at this time. This would be the occasion to ask the parent-in-training:[14]

- **Do you feel secure where you are at right now?**
- **Do you have a feeling that I understand you? Or, do you get the feeling that you are not understood adequately?**
- **Is there anything you feel uncomfortable with?**
- **How did you feel till now?**

---

14. See Navigation Sheet No. 7, p. 123.

## Third Encounter

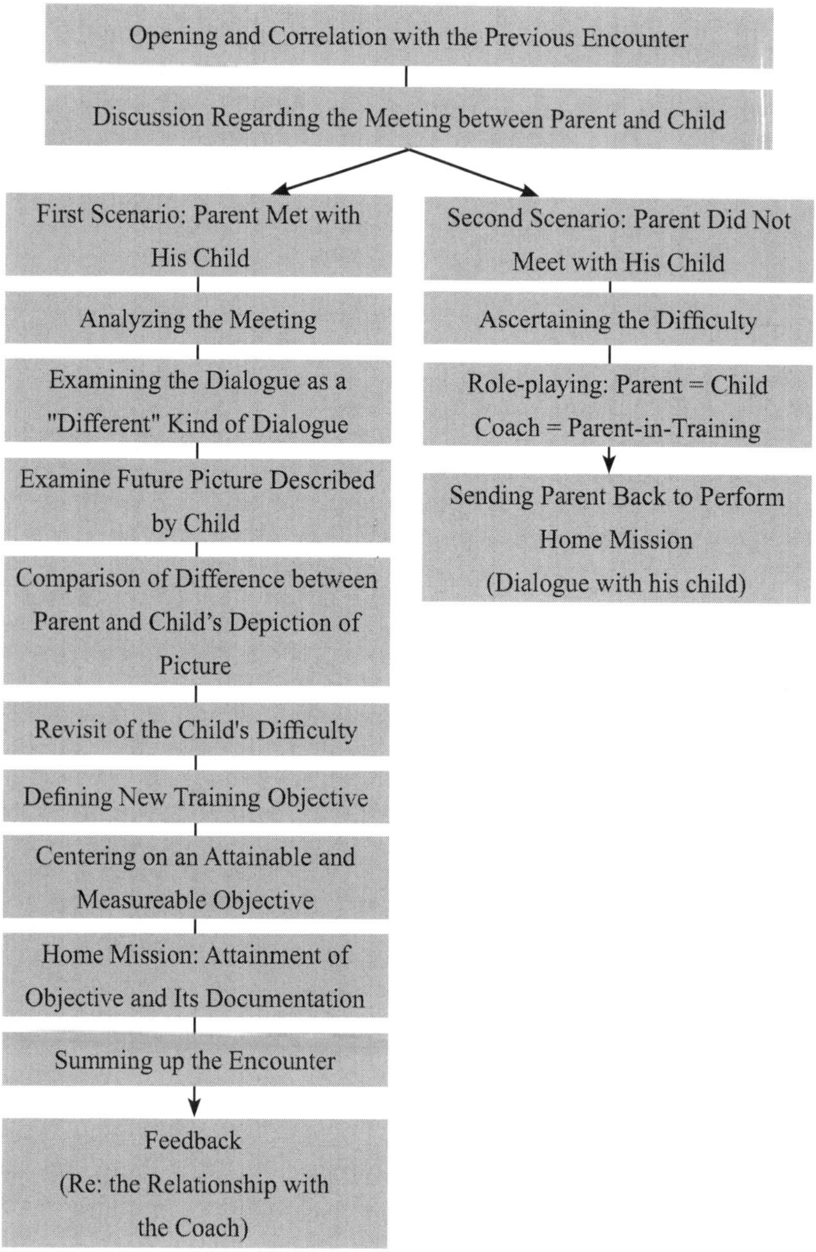

### Navigation Sheet No. 5 for the Coach

## First Step on the Path to Transformation

The coach will ask the parent-in-training the following questions and write down his words.

Why, in your role as a parent, is the chosen objective important to you?

Why is the chosen objective important to your child?

What do you expect will occur when you reach the objective?

### Navigation Sheet No. 6 for the Parent-in-Training

## The Mission to Be Performed at Home

After attaining the chosen objective, answer the following questions:

What did you do in order to attain the objective?

What were the results?

In what way, in your mind, did you progress toward attaining the training goal?

### Navigation Sheet No. 2 for the Coach

## Summary for the Parent-in-Training

We will ask the parent-in-training the following questions during the final few minutes and write down his words.

What are your insights as a result of the encounter?

________________________________________________
________________________________________________
________________________________________________
________________________________________________
________________________________________________
________________________________________________
________________________________________________
________________________________________________

Did anything strike you as particularly significant during the encounter?

________________________________________________
________________________________________________
________________________________________________
________________________________________________
________________________________________________
________________________________________________
________________________________________________
________________________________________________
________________________________________________

Is there any specific question you think I should have asked but didn't?

Is there anything you would have done differently?

Is there anything at all that you'd like to add?

**Navigation Sheet No. 7 for the Coach**

## Feedback

We will examine our interaction with the parent-in-training, and how the latter feels about the training space at this juncture. We will write down his words.

Do you feel secure where you are at right now?

________________________________________
________________________________________
________________________________________
________________________________________
________________________________________
________________________________________
________________________________________
________________________________________

Do you have a feeling that I understand you? Or, do you get the feeling that you are not understood adequately?

________________________________________
________________________________________
________________________________________
________________________________________
________________________________________
________________________________________
________________________________________
________________________________________

Is there anything you feel uncomfortable with?

How did you feel till now?

## Fourth Encounter

# The Training Goal

During this encounter, the parent-in-training will shift from defining an external training goal to outlining an internal one. During the encounter, the coach will examine the training goal in its current definition and will assist the parent-in-training to hone it in more clearly, more precisely: A goal based on objective reality that will acquire a transformative dynamic – even if at a barely perceptible level – as long as it is considered significant in regard to the inner transformation the parent-in-training is expected to undergo.

## Understanding the Steps in the Process

It is important during this encounter to clarify what has transpired so far in the training room, and the parent-in-training's position in the process.
Making the parent-in-training aware and transforming him into a full-fledged partner will assist us in reaching the desired goal, one in which inner-focus control is achieved. Understanding the steps in the definition process of the training goal and the factors that affect its formation will enable the parent-in-training to take an active role in the process from a stance of awareness and deep-sense understanding.

## The Process till Now

The three encounters till now dealt with various subjects: During the first, the parent-in-training arrived aiming to deal with his child's difficulties. In the second, we dealt with the future vision of the child, which allows the parent-in-training to have perspective in time which helps him define his goal. The third encounter is where the parent-in-training added his child's point of view to the training goal, by way of dialogue, attentiveness and closeness-enhancing communication.
Redefining the training goal enables choosing a concrete objective that serves the future picture of his child, as it is envisioned by the parent-in-training. The process he has been through till now assists

in creating new insights that pave the path toward an internal training goal.

Each one of these steps is vital to the success of the process. Therefore, if one of these steps was not performed, we will pause and complete it, jointly with the parent-in-training, in order to proceed. Thus, for instance, if the dialogue with the child was not accomplished, we ask the parent-in-training to repeat it; without it the process is incomplete, for we have left the child behind.

## Milestones

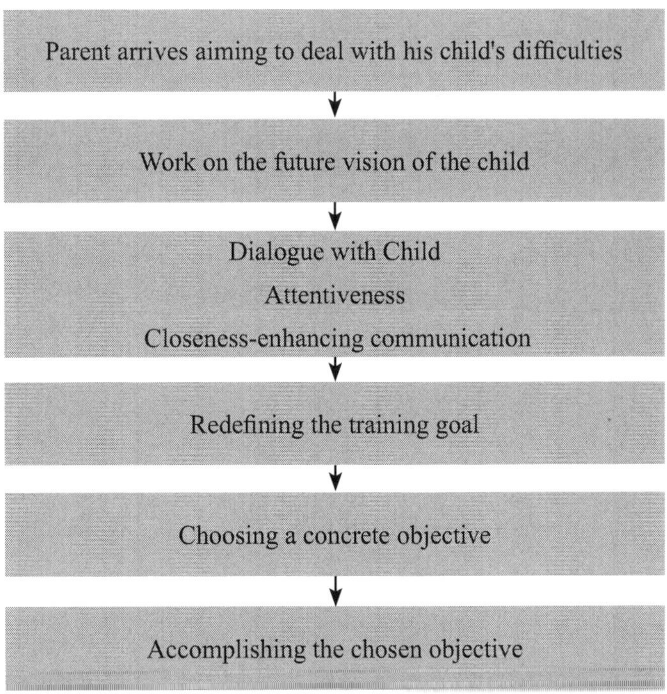

## Focusing on the Chosen Objective

This encounter gets us to center on the chosen objective, which propels the parent-in-training and provides him with impetus for change. Accomplishing the objective allows a nestling confidence to grow in the parent's heart that he can bring about positive results to his child's life and encourage him to choose additional, achievable objectives that bring him closer to the desired goal: the one that led him to seek training in the first place.

The chosen objective must be such that it will lead to a shift – as minor as it might be – that will be considered significant for him.

## Analysis of the Chosen Objective

The chosen objective does not constitute the final goal of the parent-in-training; however, it elucidates the way he would function as a rule. Accordingly, we will ask:

- **How did you conduct yourself?**
- **What has served to assist you?**
- **What has served to promote your undertaking?**
- **What has blocked you?**
- **What is it that you want to achieve?**

A deep understanding of the course of action preferred by the parent-in-training and an acquisition of in-depth knowledge of relevant details enables further development and further refinement of the inner training goal.

## Redefining the Training Goal

We will take the parent-in-training to the initial definition of the training goal, the one with which he arrived at the first encounter, and then through its evolution till this stage in the process. The replay from the start through the training goal's refinement at this point allows him to experience its progression till now – this is what fuels the training process.

We will ask: "**Does the training goal's definition remain unaffected – or does it change as a result of the process so far?** "

If the goal remained the same since the start of the process, we will ask: "**What, in the process you've been through, has strengthened you? What was it that contributed to your strengthening?**"

If the goal has changed, however, we will inquire: "**What, in the process you've been through, has brought about the change in goal definition?**"

The training goal cannot be too general; there is a need for concrete examples to demonstrate why it, specifically, was picked by the parent. This is an opportunity to return to the chosen objective and enable the parent-in-training to observe the specific difficulty in a wider context.

The coach's aim is to proceed toward a training goal that is defined in a more convergent manner and is

rooted in objective ground – not to remain at the starting point where training commenced.
It is important to work with the parent on what *he* considers important – as opposed to implanting a goal the coach regards as proper and worthy.

## Shirley's Training Goal

As a mother to a child with significant challenges, Shirley had set, during the first encounter, this goal: *"I want to learn how I can better help Yaron, how I can support his progress and how we can avoid losing precious time."*
In her future vision she was able to see Yaron at his high school commencement, mature and independent, singing with everybody else on stage at the ceremony. As a result of what she had envisioned, she redefined her training goal, to clarify: *"How can I help Yaron to become mature, independent and surrounded by friends?"*
At the third encounter Shirley was sent to form a dialogue with Yaron regarding his TV watching (specifically, a reality program, called *Big Brother*, which Yaron watched religiously). The endless preoccupation with the program was highly disturbing to Shirley. She had now decided to watch it with her son, in an attempt to understand: What did he see that was so intriguing? Why was the program so significant for him, since he spoke about it so affectionately?
By jointly watching, Shirley sought to penetrate

her son's inner world and get acquainted with other aspects of his person, those that want her "to be with him" as opposed to "do with him."

By listening to her son, Shirley discovered a whole world she did not know existed: From an episode where discussion ensued in the reality show about treachery among friends and "a knife in the back," a dialogue evolved between mother and son about the significance of friendship and loyalty to friends. Is it permissible to betray a friend, and if so then when? Did he ever betray a friend? Did she?

Shirley learned that through *Big Brother*, a program she was so strongly opposed to, her son was learning about social situations and relationships among people – an area in which he experienced difficulties in his own life. Watching the program together, and the subsequent discussion, clarified Shirley's understanding of the show's value for her son and why it was significant for him. Reaching the chosen objective, with the assistance of queries by the coach, allowed the mother to look inwardly and develop the understanding that less is more, that there is a need to shift from "doing" to "being," that the reality show has become a joint experience for mother and son and served as a means for the mother to discuss various social situations with her son, to get closer to him and better understand his inner world.

From these insights, there may be derived (in this, fourth encounter) a training goal with an inner-focus control. Such would let Shirley control the nearly impossible reality she experienced day in and day out, and help her be in a place of lessened activity, be more relaxed, serene and confident that she is doing the right thing for her child.

The training goal started evolving when the mother sought tools and knowledge that could be of assistance for her child's healthy growth – a goal with an external focal control point. It then acquired inner-focus control, where the mother let go her incessant doing in favor of being, of presence with her son. In this way, Shirley is attuned to her son's inner world and gives him the space to be himself, dynamically growing along his own self-path. Ironically, this magical zone, where the mother does less, is what enables her son to form social bonds with his peers.

## Transition From External to Internal Training Goal

In this encounter, we seek to transition control from an externally focused (depending on others) to an internal one (depending on oneself). This occurs as the parent-in-training observes his behavioral patterns and explores his own inner realm.

The inner goal can be discerned in the gap between what the parent-in-training has been doing, till now, and what he will be doing henceforth.

We will inquire: "**What is it that you have to do differently now in order to accomplish the objective you have chosen?**"

Even when the parent-in-training understands the 'why' as to what he has to do and the 'what' he must undertake, the crux of his challenge is embodied in the 'how,' i.e., a conversion of knowledge into comprehensive action.

| External focal control | Internal focal control |
|---|---|
| *"It's out of my control."* | *"I assume responsibility for my life."* <br> *"I am in charge of . . ."* |
| *"This child must change his ways."* | *"The change starts with me."* |
| *"The school fails to adequately address the matter."* | *"How do I enlist the school to support my child?"* |

## Tranquil With My Child

Initially, when Gali came to receive training, her goal was to make her family more cohesive. She really wanted to help her son, Ido, to be rid of the pressures he was under. She wanted to make things easier for him emotionally and academically. Her goal kept evolving: *"To know how to help Ido with his homework so that he will get a fair shake; to know how to guide him unerringly; to help alleviate his stresses and fears of the unknown; to get him to stop being anxious; and to get him to loosen up."* The goal underwent a significant transformation, and became the mother's internalized goal: *"To be a lot less stressed when I function in family settings. To learn to cope with my own anxieties and pressures, and to alleviate my stress so that I am in control, not it (the stress)."* Gali identifies the common denominator she shares with her son and realizes that only its alleviation will bring home tranquility and composure. She realizes that her stress affects and pressures others around her. In choosing a minor objective, en route to the overall training goal, she opted, despite the challenge entailed, *"to screen calls in order to be with my child – not to jump every time the phone rings and tune him out. I want to reach the qualitative state of being with him tranquilly."* After accomplishing her objective, Ido repeatedly told her how much he enjoys spending an afternoon with her.

## In-Depth Understanding of The Internal Training Goal

This encounter is the continuation of the process where the parent-in-training redefines his initial training goal, the one that brought him to seek training. The coach works with the parent-in-training and assists him to center on an internal training goal, and to figure out how he can form new behavioral patterns.

Frequently, it is hard for the parent-in-training to identify the pattern that effects a block in his life, and to explain where else he encounters it – apart from his interaction with his child.

Sifting through issues and outlooks (perceptions) that interfere with the parent-in-training's participation in the process allows discernment of the gap between the difficulty and its assorted expressions. The parent-in-training brings with him inner noise – for he is emotionally flooded, thus unable to clearly attune to veiled aspects of the self that direct his conduct as he interacts with his child (which often runs his own life in the same unconscious manner).

The coach, therefore, ought to take the parent out of the enclosed training room and place him in a setting of his daily activity by asking:

**"This difficulty that came up in your interaction with your child – where else do you run into it in your daily life?"**

We will ask the parent-in-training to illustrate, in minute detail.

We then will further inquire, for instance:

- **In your mind, what was the reason for your inability to cope effectively with the challenge you're facing? What in your opinion had limited you?**

- **What is it or who is it – in your opinion – that could be of assistance to you in order to effectively cope with the challenge you're facing?**
- **Describe yourself without that difficulty. How do you see your child's life if this difficulty were done away with?**
- **Who's aid did you enlist in handling this difficulty till now? How do others (e.g., family members) relate to this difficulty?**

## Strengthening the Parent in Future Encounters

The training goal will be reexamined time and again during subsequent encounters as we endeavor to enhance the parent's empowerment model and his child's values. We will know that we have reached the right place with coherence, consistency and harmony between the training goal on one hand, and the parent and his child's viewpoint on the other hand have been reached while putting an emphasis on the strengths of all parties involved.

This encounter is highly significant, and at times will require more than one meeting in order to reach a training goal with internal focus of control. The Home Mission purpose is to seek to establish what has been learned in the current encounter and enable the parent-in-training to undergo a process of reflection where he will sort out the experiences he went through in the training room.

We will ask the parent-in-training to answer these questions:[15]

- **Is there something new you have learned about yourself today? If so, please explain in detail.**
- **Where do you come across what you have learned (in this encounter) in other areas of your life (work, family life, socially, etc.)?**

## Summation for the Parent-in-Training

During the last few minutes of the encounter the parent-in-training will answer *Summation Questions for the Parent-in-Training*:[16]

- **What are your insights as a result of the encounter?**
- **Did anything strike you as particularly significant during the encounter?**
- **Is there any specific question you think I should have asked but didn't?**
- **Is there anything you would have done differently?**
- **Is there anything at all that you'd like to add?**

15. See Navigation Sheet No. 8, p. 139.

16. See Navigation Sheet No. 2, p. 140.

# Fourth Encounter

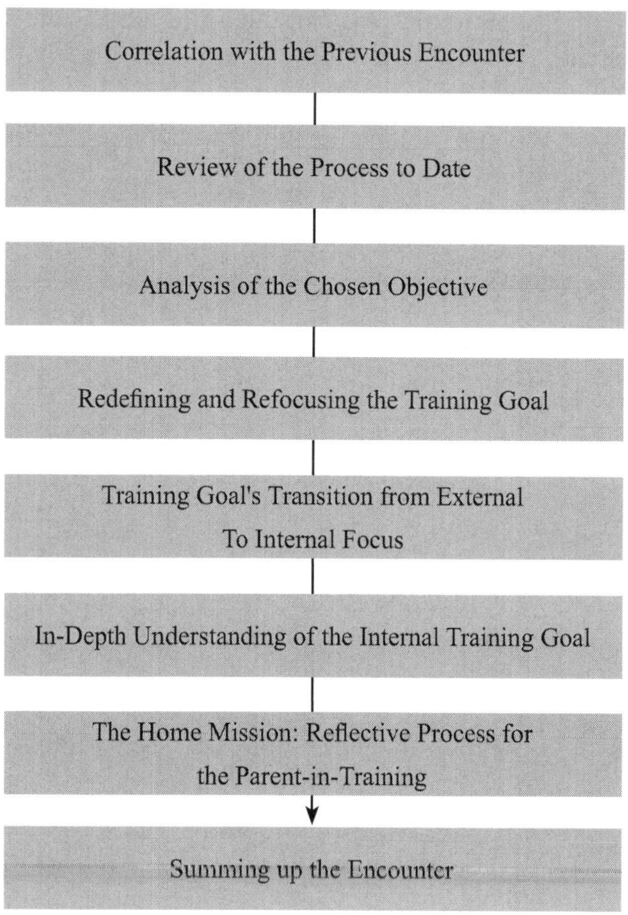

### Navigation Sheet No. 8 for the Parent-in-Training

## The Home Mission

Think about the process you went through in this training encounter and answer the following questions:

Is there something new you have learned about yourself today? If so, please explain.

Where do you come across what you have learned (in this encounter) in other areas of your life (work, family life, socially, etc.)?

### Navigation Sheet No. 2 for the Coach

## Summary for the Parent-in-Training

We will ask the parent-in-training the following questions during the final few minutes and write down his words.

What are your insights as a result of the encounter?

______________________________

______________________________

______________________________

______________________________

______________________________

______________________________

______________________________

______________________________

______________________________

Did anything strike you as particularly significant during the encounter?

______________________________

______________________________

______________________________

______________________________

______________________________

______________________________

______________________________

______________________________

Is there any specific question you think I should have asked but didn't?

Is there anything you would have done differently?

Is there anything at all that you'd like to add?

## Fifth Encounter

# Empowerment Model

During this encounter, the parent-in-training learns about himself: about his strength and weaknesses, apprehensions, threats that manifest in his reality and the opportunities embodied in all these. Through stories taken out of his life, the coach brings the parent-in-training to meet both the successes and failures he has been through, thus allowing him to gain a valuable insight – that a given difficulty can serve as a challenge of great significance in the process of developing coping skills (regarding his child).

## The Empowerment Model

The empowerment model used in the training process is based on a model from the business world, known as the *SWOT Model*, which is designed to examine the corporate strengths and weaknesses as compared to business rivals and competitors, and to assess opportunities and peril lurking in the corporate environment.
The term is an acronym of its four components:

**S**- Strengths

**W** – Weaknesses

**O** – Opportunities

**T** – Threats & Fears

## Using the Empowerment Model in the Training Process

Utilization of the empowerment model during the training process allows the parent-in-training to identify his strengths, his fears and perceived threats as well as opportunities that, at present, go unnoticed. During this encounter we will make use of the empowerment model in order to map its four aspects as they relate to the interaction between the parent-in training and his child.

## The Parent's Empowerment Model

| Promoting Factors | Delaying Factors |
|---|---|
| **Strengths** | **Weaknesses** |
| **Opportunities** | **Threats (External)** |
| | **Fears (Internal)** |

## Samples

**Strengths**: Empathy, sensitivity, patience, determination, creativity, responsibility, independence, order and organization, sincerity, generosity.
**Weaknesses**: Impatience, helplessness, inflexibility, uncommunicative, moodiness, impulsiveness, passivity.
**Fears** (internal): of failure, of rejection, of loss of authority, of loss of love.
**Threats** (external): that the child will be kicked out of school, that he will be rejected by society, that he will hook up with a fringe group, that he will not be able to secure employment, that he won't be able to establish a family, that he won't succeed in becoming mature and independent.
**Opportunities**: to become a better parent, to become a more attentive and understanding partner (in a relationship), to experience love, to learn a particular aspect of life because of the child, thus

enrich oneself, to be able to lend a hand to other parents in the same circumstances.

## Coping Stories – When I Was Successful

In order to map strengths in the empowerment model, we will ask the parent-in-training: "**Try to recall an event you experienced as a success in your life: Something either from your work, school, or some other area.**"

After we have heard his story, we will ask: "**What strengths came into play in this story?**"

We will assist the parent-in-training to discover his strengths – including the ones veiled from his awareness – that nonetheless made an appearance in his story. The coach will write down the expressions of strength, using the parent's words, in the applicable space in the empowerment model.[17]

Explain to the parent-in-training that, on many occasions, difficulties and the sense of helplessness might cause us to forget our strengths and the purpose of training is to help him rediscover them.

---

17. See Navigation Sheet No. 9, p. 162.

## Red Hot Chili Café

Shosh imparted a success story about setting up a business, a café named "Red Hot Chili." *"I established it thirty years ago. I was young, a college student with no experience in such matters. I did things intuitively, from an innate sense of what's the right thing to do and what's not. These days there are programs set up to teach entrepreneurship and how to run a business. There were things that I simply knew were the right things to do. I have this inborn insight of what's correct ... not from books or according to a set formula. ... The café became a popular hangout, because it had my spirit imbued in it."*

When asked what she saw as the essence of her success, she replied: *"To give a client service and create an ambiance of uncommon quality; to create exceptional standards, superb by all parameters ... to create a kind of a unique culture...."*

When asked what helped her succeed, she said: *"Success is the ability to notice myriad details simultaneously. Success happened because I saw human beings in front of me and attended to each one personally; to remember what each one has been through – attentiveness!!! The ability to get staff into action. To manage and understand how things should be handled."*

Shosh then listed a number of strengths she recognized having: *"An ability to manage and to mobilize, attention to detail, intelligence, personal attention to others – an ability to ascertain what will make another (a customer) feel at ease, an ability to organize, authoritative yet capable of delegating authority, communicative, articulate, efficient, caring, perfectionist, an ability to be in charge, decisiveness and analytical ability."*

## A Story of Failure to Cope – When I Didn't Succeed

We will ask the parent-in-training: "**Try and remember an event you've experienced during your life as one of failure; either something from your work, school or some other area.**"
After we have heard his story, we will ask: "**What weaknesses came into play in this story? What were the fear and threats you've experienced?**"
We will help him discover his weaknesses, fears and the threats that loom over him – even those he is unaware of – the ones that made an appearance in his story. The coach will write down the expressions of weaknesses, fears and threats, using the parent's words, in the applicable space in the empowerment model.

## Shosh's Fears and Threats

When asked about her fears and the threats she feels looming in her life, Shosh replied: "*There was an article about me in a newspaper which said that, at the end of each shift, I use toothpicks to make sure that the openings in the saltshakers are not blocked. It was used to illustrate my tendency to insure that all is in order to the smallest detail. It is an example of the exacting standards I maintain ... the price is an exhaustion I didn't recover from."*

Shosh enumerated her weaknesses: *"I waste energy (resources), I'm authoritarian – I expect people to act on my whims – I need to be in control, I am too particular, perfectionist."*

As to threats, she said: *"I'm threatened by the sense that everything is transient – all that success ... that soon my bluff will be called...."*

About fears she said: *"I have an existential anxiety, economic survival...."*

As to opportunities, she stated: *"I seek an opening to release those around me – and myself – of my need for perfectionism, of the waste of energy on trivial matters, to have perspective on things, to get less excited. Create less drama in my life."*

## Strengths as Weaknesses and Weaknesses as Strengths

We will explain to the parent-in-training that sometimes a weakness is a strength and vice versa. There are neither positive nor negative aspects. Likewise, fears and threats could serve as opportunities to expand our coping ability and transform a difficulty into a challenge.

For instance, sensitivity could often be interpreted as a weakness, yet in the context of the parent-in-training's relationship with his child, sensitivity is a strong point and an advantage, which enables deeper insight into the experience of difficulty the child undergoes. It is this quality that summons up an intimate meeting that boosts the child. When the parent harnesses his sensitivity to the interaction with his child, such quality is an advantage that assists him to feel empathy and converse with his child, who then feels that he is heard, that he is emotionally held by the parent and that he has value in the parent's eyes. In contrast, the presence of sensitivity in a different setting, e.g., making rational decisions at one's place of work, could manifest as a weakness.

## Weakness and Difficulty As Opportunity

We will ask the parent-in-training: "**During our encounters you've described numerous difficulties; however, many times we learn that opportunities can emerge out of crisis and struggle. Do you identify an opportunity affecting your life? Affecting you personally? What out of this process could constitute an opportunity for you?**"
It is the role of the coach to promote the parent-in-training's understanding that difficulties and crises are actually a process where he fosters his ability to cope with challenges. The challenge entailed enables him to realize the significance of different components in his life, such as: the meaning of parenthood of a child with disabilities, relationship (with a mate), family life and employment.

Time and again the parent-in-training struggles when he seeks to bring about a change in his personal life. However, our personal experience teaches us that when what is at stake could impact his child's well-being, he is willing, unselfishly, to do what he can to effect the change. When the anticipated change brings with it success into the child's life, other aspects of the parent's life improve as well.

The process of coping with one's child's learning disabilities or attention deficit disorder summons a learning experience into the parent's life. When such trial is perceived as significant, the parent sees the lesson as an opportunity to learn about himself, his life and his environment, which makes it easier for him to cope with such challenge. In this event, the parent-in-training's insight grows deeper, for opportunity and growth often surface out of a crisis, exactly where the parent is apprehensive about breaking down.

Here, we will ask the parent-in-training: "**Of all the events you've described, what can you take with you as a means of coping with your child's difficulties?**"

We will assist him to unearth extant opportunities in his life.

The coach will write down these expressions, using the parent's words, in the applicable space in the empowerment model.

## Coach's Viewpoint

When Ofra brought up the subject of responsibility as a strength in her empowerment model, the coach took advantage of that in order to go deeper and inquired: *"Where else do you run into the subject of responsibility in your life?"* Ofra talked about unusual abilities she demonstrated in her volunteer activities with young people. She mainly spoke about her skills of empathy and attentiveness. When the coach brought the discussion back to the relation between the mother-in-training and her daughter, the significant difficulty the mother had in listening to and feeling empathy for her daughter surfaced. The coach sought to ascertain the difficulty in listening to her daughter in light of the fact that she had been able to demonstrate these skills in her volunteer activity.

## Enhancement of Strengths and Expansion of Opportunities

By filling out the empowerment model form the coach will help the parent-in-training to define how he can enhance his strengths and expand his opportunities for dealing with difficulties that come his way. The idea is to mobilize abilities and means: Those that have effectively served the parent in the past, which could lead to a positive change in his relationship with his child, and to an improvement in his present function as a parent.

## The Empowerment Model of Yael

Yael is a 34-year-old woman, a painter and artist who studied at Bezalel.[18] During the training sessions she frequently expressed guilt for not being a good enough mother. She claimed that often she was the only voice heard at home. She felt that, most of the time, she lost her patience all too quickly. She disclosed that she was unable to just hug her child and forgive him; that she experienced strong feelings of anger and rejection. That when she was able to contain her anger she felt great; when she didn't she was consumed with guilt.

Yael understood that she held an important key to a door that could lead to the success of her child. Even so, she felt helpless, scared and threatened, weak and too powerless to cope. The empowerment model is designed to empower Yael, give her the requisite strength, to assist her in putting her feelings in order, evoke hope in her heart by reminding her what she has already forgotten – her strengths.

After completing the mapping of her empowerment model, Yael was amazed to discover that she possessed numerous strengths, the existence of

18. Bezalel Academy of Art and Design in Jerusalem, founded in 1906, is Israel's national school of art, named for the Biblical figure Bezalel Ben Uri, appointed by Moses to oversee the design and construction of the Tabernacle (Exodus 35:30).

which she managed to forget. Now, written in black and white, they would accompany her awareness from now on.

| **Strengths** | **Weaknesses** |
|---|---|
| Love<br>Sensitivity<br>Softness<br>Resourcefulness<br>Creativity<br>Ambition<br>Determination<br>Tolerance<br>Patience<br>Appearance<br>Ability to conduct an effective dialogue<br>Foresightedness<br>Organization | Sensitivity (to noise, disorder)<br>Softness<br>Frustration with her inability to accomplish what she wants<br>Moodiness<br>Difficulty seeing the beauty in things<br>A tendency to focus on flaws<br>Inarticulate at times<br>Impulsive, short fuse, irritability |

<table>
<tr><td rowspan="2">Opportunities<br>To 'mend' myself through my child<br>To be centered in beauty<br>To let go, to relax<br>An opportunity to maintain and improve the relationship with my spouse</td><td>Threats<br>That my son might fail in school and that he'd be kicked out of school</td></tr>
<tr><td>Fears<br>Fear of failure<br>Fear of losing control over my child<br>The greatest fear – that I won't be able to bring myself to where I'll be a happy person</td></tr>
</table>

## The Empowerment Model of Yael

Insights the model has given rise to as we complete working on the empowerment model, we will ask the parent-in-training:

- **To what extent are you aware of your strengths and capable of seeing the opportunities that come your way?**
- **To what extent are you aware of and comprehend your own fears and threats, which prevent you from coping?**

## Empowerment Model of the Child

We will ask the parent-in-training to fill up all four aspects of the empowerment model for his child.[19] Remember, the use of the model is an opportunity for the parent to become aware of his child's strengths/weaknesses/fears/threats and, concurrently, to understand where he ends and where his child begins, to aid his ability to distinguish between what is his child's and what is his.

19. See Navigation Sheet No. 10, p. 163.

## The Empowerment Model from Guy's Mother's Point of View

<table>
<tr><td>Strengths<br>Determination<br>A good friend<br>Very loving – loves totally<br>Forgives easily<br>Funny – has a sense of humor<br>Independence<br>Sensitivity<br>Ambition to be a success<br>Lovely penmanship<br>An ability to save (money)</td><td>Weaknesses<br>Irresponsibility<br>Inattentiveness<br>Vulnerability<br>Dishonesty – a tendency to lie<br>A tie between money and self-esteem (as a measure of success)<br>Lack of ability to concentrate<br>Inarticulate<br>Envy and looking up to others as opposed to appreciating what he has</td></tr>
<tr><td rowspan="2">Opportunities<br>A springboard – for becoming a better child, more mature and confident – to move on to a new level</td><td>Threats (external)<br>He will be kicked out of school;<br>He won't get along in the army</td></tr>
<tr><td>Fears (internal)<br>Of threatening characters<br>Of the unknown<br>Of the dark</td></tr>
</table>

## The Home Mission:

### Part One

In the first part of the home mission we will ask the parent-in-training to conduct, during the intervening week, a dialogue with his child and ascertain how the child sees himself in relation to the four aspects of the empowerment model.[20] We will ask the parent to "translate" the empowerment model to a series of simplified questions which could assist the child to understand; in addition, we will ask the parent to utilize what transpired in the training room as a guiding tool in the present interaction with the child.

We recommend asking the child to tell a success story, in order to encourage and support his spirit.

For example, the parent-in-training could ask his child:

- **What are you good at?**
- **What area have you experienced success in?**
- **What do you think you might be less good at?**
- **What are you afraid of?**
- **What do you perceive as threatening?**

We will ask the parent-in-training to also relate to the element of *opportunities* in the discussion with his child. He could, for instance, say: *"After we have*

20. See Navigation Sheet No. 11, p. 164.

*considered your strengths, after we've discussed your weaknesses, fears and what you find threatening, do you see any opportunity in the reality you're experiencing?"* Advancing further in this dimension of opportunities is usually feasible with adolescents and adults, ripe for this stage, deeper understanding and insight of the obstacles is required and, as well as of the implied opportunities within them. When the child is able to see the challenge embedded within the difficulty, this constitutes an opportunity for development and growth in other areas of his life.

We will ask the parent-in-training not to direct the child nor guide his responses, for example, "Isn't it true that…?" but, instead, allow the child to express himself unaided and unguided. We will, however, instruct the parent to utilize closeness-enhancing communication.

**Part Two**

We will explain to the parent-in-training that in the second part of the mission to be performed at home, he will be asked to compare the child's empowerment model from the parent's viewpoint (the one he had prepared during the current encounter) with the empowerment model he had produced from his child's success story during the dialogue between them. We will ask the parent-in-training to write the following:

**"What are the differences among the model's four**

**aspects? What did you learn from this comparison?**[21]

## A Successful Meeting

At the conclusion of a successful meeting, the parent-in-training feels empowered and reinforced. He feels that he has acquired abilities and tools and consequently, that he now owns the strengths required in order to cope with the difficulties he has been experiencing.

## Summation for the Parent-in-Training

During the last few minutes of the encounter the parent-in-training will answer the *Summation Questions for the Parent-in-Training*,[22] as follows:

- **What are your insights as a result of the encounter?**
- **Did anything strike you as particularly significant during the encounter?**
- **Is there any specific question you think I should have asked but didn't?**
- **Is there anything you would have done differently?**
- **Is there anything at all that you'd like to add?**

---

21. See Navigation Sheet No. 12, p. 166.

22. See Navigation Sheet No. 2, p. 168.

# Fifth Encounter

Opening and Correlation with the Previous Encounter

Explanation of the Empowerment Model & Its Importance

Mapping the Parent-in-Training's Strengths with Stories of Success

Mapping Weaknesses, Fears and Threats with Stories of Lack of Success

Explanation: Weaknesses as Strengths & Strengths as Weaknesses

Identifying Opportunities

Examining Insights Found in the Empowerment Model

Mapping the Empowerment Model of the Child by the Parent-in-Training

The Home Mission:

- Mapping the Empowerment Model of the Child in His Own Eyes
- Comparing the Empowerment Model: from both the child and the parent's point of view

Summing up the Encounter

### Navigation Sheet No. 9 for the Coach

## Empowerment Model of the Parent-in-Training

The coach will write down the expressions of weaknesses, strengths, threats, fears and opportunities, using the parent's words, in the applicable space in the empowerment model.

<table>
<tr><td>Strengths</td><td>Weaknesses</td></tr>
<tr><td rowspan="2">Opportunities</td><td>Threats (External)</td></tr>
<tr><td>Fears (Internal)</td></tr>
</table>

### Navigation Sheet No. 10 for the Coach

## Empowerment Model of the Child (From the Parent-in-Training's Viewpoint)

The parent-in-training will map the four aspects of the empowerment model in relation to his child. He will write the various expressions that come to his mind in the right space of the table below.

| **Strengths** | **Weaknesses** |
|---|---|
| **Opportunities** | **Threats (External)** |
| | **Fears (Internal)** |

### Navigation Sheet No. 11 for the Parent-in-Training

## Empowerment Model of the Child (From his Viewpoint)

Conduct a dialogue with your child during the week and find out: How does he see himself? How does he express the four aspects of the empowerment model?

Transliterate the empowerment model to simple inquiries which your child can comprehend. Ask him to tell you a success story. For instance, you could ask such questions:

- **What are you good at?**
- **What area have you experienced success in?**
- **What do you think you might be less good at?**
- **What are you afraid of?**
- **What do you perceive as threatening in your life?**

A reminder: Don't direct the child or guide his responses, for example, "Isn't it true that…?" but, instead, allow the child to express himself unaided and unguided, using closeness-enhancing communication.

<table>
<tr><td>Strengths</td><td>Weaknesses</td></tr>
<tr><td rowspan="2">Opportunities</td><td>Threats (External)</td></tr>
<tr><td>Fears (Internal)</td></tr>
</table>

### Navigation Sheet No. 12 for the Parent-in-Training

## The Child's Empowerment Model
## Part Two of the Home Mission

Compare the child's empowerment model from your point of view (the one you have mapped out during the current encounter) to the empowerment model from his viewpoint (the one you have mapped out following the meeting with him).

Write down the differences in regard to each aspect of the model, and tell us what you have learned from the exercise.

| | **There was a difference.** | **There wasn't a difference.** | **What have you learned from the comparison?** |
|---|---|---|---|
| Strengths | | | |

| | There was a difference. | There wasn't a difference. | What have you learned from the comparison? |
|---|---|---|---|
| Weaknesses | | | |
| Threats | | | |
| Fears | | | |
| Opportunities | | | |

### Navigation Sheet No. 2 for the Coach

## Summary for the Parent-in-Training

We will ask the parent-in-training the following questions during the final few minutes and write down his words.

What are your insights as a result of the encounter?

_______________________________________________

_______________________________________________

_______________________________________________

_______________________________________________

_______________________________________________

_______________________________________________

_______________________________________________

_______________________________________________

_______________________________________________

Did anything strike you as particularly significant during the encounter?

_______________________________________________

_______________________________________________

_______________________________________________

_______________________________________________

_______________________________________________

_______________________________________________

_______________________________________________

_______________________________________________

Is there any specific question you think I should have asked but didn't?

Is there anything you would have done differently?

Is there anything at all that you'd like to add?

## Sixth Encounter

# To What Do I Say "Yes" and to What Do I Say "No"?

During the first part of this encounter we will compare the empowerment model of the parent-in-training to that of the child.
During the second part we will assist the parent-in-training to enhance his awareness about the values guiding him in life, by presenting the following question: To what do I say "Yes" and to what do I say "No"? Thus, the parent develops insights that help him see both aspects of the value in which he believes, and comprehend that there are no absolute values.

## The Empowerment Model of the Child

At the start of the encounter we will inquire with the parent-in-training about the home mission he received during the previous encounter, and ask if he was able to conduct a dialogue with his child about his strengths, weaknesses, opportunities, fears and the threats he perceives.

Parents-in-training experience their children subjectively. They believe that they know what the child feels/thinks and what he might want. The parent-in-training sees his child through his own eyes, thus he is unable to experience the objective reality his child is experiencing. Indeed, the child can often fathom what is expected of him and behaves accordingly, without remaining loyal to his own self. Even when the parent-in-training thinks himself empathetic toward his child and that he understands him, such is insufficient in order to realize where the child is at and truly experience what the child really goes through. These are cases where it is difficult to create a separation between the parent-in-training and the child. As the parent undergoes the training, he learns to conduct a dialogue with his child from a place of "I do not know," or "I am unfamiliar." He remains curious and learns more and more about and from his child in a dynamic process: one that never ends.

In this process, the child discovers things he did not know about himself. Likewise, the parent-in-training unearths what has been previously hidden from his perception. This new way commences when the parent-in-training says: "I didn't know," and the child discovers new insights about himself. It's the start of a new, challenging journey on a path that the parent-in-training and his child have not yet traversed.

## Two Possible Scenarios

There are two possible scenarios:

1. The parent-in-training did conduct a dialogue with his child about the empowerment model.
2. The parent-in-training did not conduct a dialogue with his child about the empowerment model.

## Scenario No. 1: The Parent-in-Training Did Conduct a Dialogue With His Child

We will ask the parent-in-training to tell us the success story his child shared with him, and the consequent conversation they conducted thereafter. We will ask:

- **Was the child aware of his strengths and weaknesses?**

- **Despite the success, could the child discuss his fears? The threats that affect him? And, the opportunities vested in the challenge he is facing?**

## Differences Between Points of View

The coach will examine with the parent-in-training the differences between the various components of the empowerment model: as they were experienced by the parent-in-training, and as they were experienced by the child. The parent-in-training should notice how his child perceives himself and the difficulties he is facing, the resulting part unrevealed to the parent, but now illuminated. He will tell the coach about those insights he has developed once he has completed the home mission.[23]

## Shiri's Empowerment Model

When, during the fifth encounter, Batya had mapped out the empowerment model of her daughter, Shiri, she described it as follows:
Strengths: Has a good heart, paints well, has a sense of humor, sings well, good with computers.

---

23. Use Navigation Sheet No. 12, p. 166. which the parent-in-training filled out at home prior to the encounter.

Weaknesses: Oversensitive, squanders, has difficulties being orderly and organized.
Threats: Disappointments from elements in her environment, violence at school.
Fears: To fail, that she will not be loved.
Opportunities: She has the ability to work with children.
After completing the home mission she disclosed: *"I found it interesting to see what Shiri had written about strengths, weaknesses, threats and opportunities – compared to what I thought. I felt that by working on this model, I started to get to know my daughter better."*
With her mother's assistance, Shiri mapped out the empowerment model in the following manner:
Strengths: Has a talent for painting, work with computers (graphics), and is good at sports (basketball and running).
Weaknesses: Overly generous, dreamy, not sufficiently considerate.
Threats: Feels threatened by certain male and female classmates.
Fears: None mentioned
Opportunities: To draw giant comics, to be on a basketball team, to design posters for school using Photoshop.

## Zohar's Empowerment Model – Learning and Insights

Eti says: *"I have regarded Zohar with a wider perspective … not just looking at one area, a much broader outlook. He relates to himself through a very narrow prism. I see the big picture, as far as he is concerned. I see for him much more than he can see for himself … at least at this stage … part of it is a matter of experience, process and age … I understand that Zohar opted to relate to a specific area. At the moment it is much harder for him to see opportunities … maybe he sees them but does not express what he sees in words. Maybe it's his age and maybe it's his way (of doing things) …."*

## Scenario No. 2: The Parent-in-Training Did Not Conduct a Dialogue With His Child

The dialogue of the parent-in-training with his child is necessary in order to enable progress in the training. When the parent-in-training is unable to conduct a dialogue with his child, the coach will endeavor to ascertain the reasons for it. It may be that the lack of implementation is caused by technical issues that have prevented holding the encounter. It is also possible that the parent-in-training came across a mission that, though it appeared simple, he found difficult to execute. Often, the parent-in-training feels that he needs additional coaching and exercise. In such a case, we will ask him to reconstruct a successful encounter he has had with his child in the past. We will map out, with the assistance of that account, the strengths and abilities of his child. With additional accounts we will assist the parent to map out other dimensions of the empowerment model, relating to weaknesses, fears, threats and opportunities of his child.

## Return to the Training Goal

As an outcome of each of the scenarios we will go back and work on the training goal; we will reinforce the learning accomplished through the use of the empowerment model, since now he understands the strengths and weaknesses of his child, is aware of his fears and the threats he perceives, and acts from a place where he is better able to identify opportunities and maximize his activities.

## Values

During the second part of the encounter we will explain to the parent-in-training that every person has a set of supreme values, according to which he conducts his life. These often appear as a judge, with a grim expression, who passes judgment and sees life in black and white (right-wrong, good-evil).

This encounter allows the exposure of the supreme values that conduct his life, bringing them to his awareness and carrying out a dialogue with them so that he is able to see all the colors of the rainbow, all the opportunities he can avail himself of and his freedom of choice.

## The Circle of Values

In utilizing the Circle of Values, we will assist the parent-in-training in identifying his behavioral patterns and the values by which he conducts himself.
We will ask: **"What are the values most important for you?"**
We will ask the parent to ponder, what the seven most significant values are in his eyes, and then write them in the Circle of Values.[24] Of the seven, we will ask the parent to mark the two he considers the most important, and to describe an event in his life where one or both values found expression in a meaningful manner.

24. See Navigation Sheet No. 13, p. 190.

**Example:**

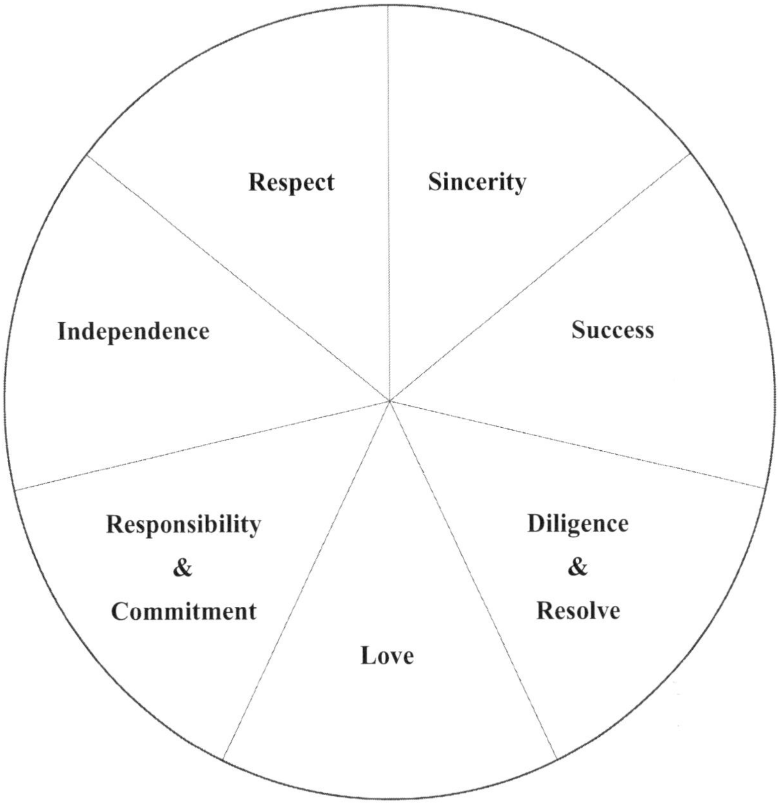


Examples of other such values are: Self-esteem, gentleness, seriousness, perseverance, affection, integrity/honesty, discipline, gratefulness, serenity, belonging, self-acceptance and more.

## Typical Coping Accounts

Ask the parent-in-training to tell you about situations of dealing with his child. Examine what he said "Yes" to and what he said "No" to in his reactions.

The parent-in-training does not need to tell a particularly dramatic account of a struggle; indeed, a typical, everyday story would be preferable.

## The Yin & Yang of The Circle of Values

Observing values through the prism is based on the view of yin and yang in ancient Chinese philosophy and metaphysics. These are two complementary forces which, contemporaneously, oppose each other. When the parent-in-training relates to a particular value, the coach's aim is to assist and examine this particular value and to help him acquire the ability to look at the value in which he believes from both its sides and ask himself:

**In a given situation, to which value do I say "Yes" and to which value do I say "No"?**

This question will assist the coach to present before the parent-in-training an additional dimension to allow him to comprehend what guides him as a parent. We will explain to him that as parents it is important for us to understand that when we say "Yes" to a particular value, we simultaneously say "No" to another value.

## Clarification Examples
## For the Coach

When I demand that my child do his homework immediately upon his return from school:

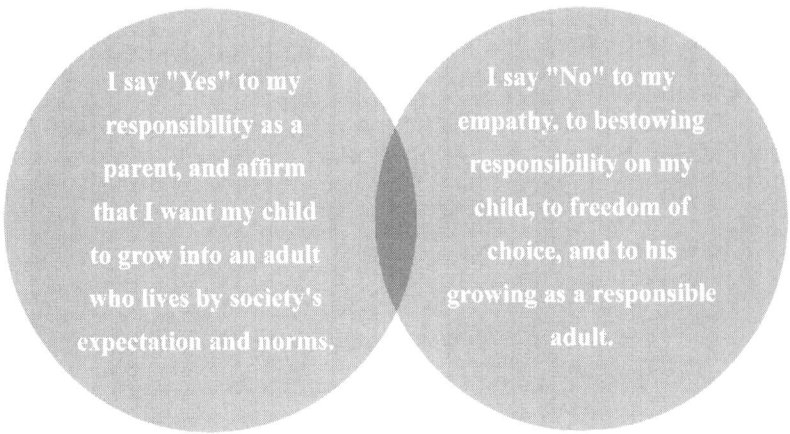


## When to Go to Sleep

Hanna said: *"When I allow my child to go to sleep whenever she wants to, I say 'Yes' to my tolerance, to my empathetic ability, and to freedom of choice – at the same time, I say 'No' to my concern for her rest so that she can go to school alert and attentive, and I say 'No' to my authority as a parent."*

## Orit Wanted a Dog

Danny told us: *"Orit wanted a dog, but I didn't agree (we had one in the past and I ended up having to care for it). She brought home a small puppy when I was not at home. I got really mad and informed her that she must take him out of the house. A few days later, she gave it to the neighbors; however, they neglected it. Orit could not stand seeing it suffer and, frankly, neither could I, and she brought it back. I sought a way to solve the problem. I shared my dilemma with her; we published an ad and found a family that would take it in. It was hard for both Orit and me, and I tried to encourage her. The values I cherished on that occasion were sensitivity, kindness to animals, cooperation, humanism, love and giving.*

*"What did I say 'Yes' to? – to my parental authority, to standing behind my decision and to cooperation in finding a solution for the problem.*

*"What did I say 'No' to? – to freedom of choice, to transferring responsibility to her and to consideration of her wishes."*

## Daniela Wants to Buy a Motorcycle

Shlomo told the following: *"Daniela worked for a short while, and saved a little money. She asked me for money for all kinds of things, such as computer repair. I then discovered an envelope stuffed with money in her room. When I asked her about it, she told me that she had placed money in there in order to purchase a motorcycle for herself. That was the last thing I was willing to hear about, and she knows it. I got really mad and felt that she was deceiving me, that she does whatever she*

*wants and lies about it. Naturally, a fight developed. The values I consider important are integrity, trust, sincerity, not taking risks and no consideration for the other.*
*"What did I say, 'Yes' to? – to my parental authority, to my responsibility as a parent, to the value of avoiding risks.*
*"What did I say 'No' to? – to deception, to lying, to transferring responsibility to Daniela, to her freedom of choice, to her sense of independence, to her wishes, to my empathy."*

## Shai Avoids Doing Homework

Amichai told us: *"Shai had homework which he avoided doing. He said he was tired, didn't know (the material), didn't want to do it and was uncooperative. I insisted that he sit down and do his homework despite all the evasive action. I added that only when he had completed his homework would he be able to hang out with his buddies in the afternoon.*
*"What did I say 'Yes' to? – to perseverance, persistence, completion of a mission and achievement. "What did I say 'No' to? – to giving up, to flexibility, to mediocrity, to Shai's choice, to pleasure and to fun."*

## Value Assessment

We will ask the parent-in-training: **What is the source of these values? Do the values dictate to**

**you a black and white course of conduct – or is there room for seeing all the colors of the rainbow?**

## The Child's Viewpoint

We will assist the parent-in-training to acquire the understanding that on many occasions he operates from an unequal stance, and try to demonstrate to him the child's view of things. We will ask him, "**What do you think the child thinks/feels?**"

It is crucial to convey to him that the child, too, has his own values, which are affected by his environment and his peer group. During certain ages the peer group often has greater influence over the child than his parents.

Often, the parent operates from within the context of his own values and his own reality. At times, what appears to be highly valuable to him is of little, if any, value to his child. This could be, and often is, a source of conflict among competing values. Thus, the parent should understand that his child is not necessarily rebellious, contradictory or flippant; instead, in many cases, he feels misunderstood. Only a meeting that accords equal place to the values of both the child and parent could lead to a true conversation that enables bridging the gaps between them.

## Instilling Values in Your Child

We will ask the parent-in-training:
**"What, in your eyes, are the essential values when it comes to educating your child?"**
We will ask the parent-in-training to choose the two most important values to him. If he did not choose them previously, he may now add them to the Circle of Values.[25]
We will then ask him to describe an event in his life in which one or both of those values had a significant effect.
We now will ask the parent-in-training: **"When you relate to these values, which one do you say 'Yes' to and which one do you say 'No' to?"**
When the parent-in-training comprehends what he says "Yes" and "No" to, and explains the rationale for his action, using the values that guide him, we will ask him: **"From the list of values to which you say 'Yes,' which one is the most significant for you? And from the list of values to which you say 'No,' which one is the most significant for you?"**
This is our opportunity to ascertain what association exists among these significant values; to what degree they assist him; and to what extent they form an inefficient pattern, causing him to exhibit undesired behavior.

---

25. See Navigation Sheet No. 13, p. 190.

## Determination as a Supreme Value

Of all the values in the circle, Noam chose determination as the most imperative value for her. When asked to describe an event in her life in which determination came into effect, she described how she had decided to bring a child into the world despite health risks and trepidation about her survival of a pregnancy. When asked by the coach what she said "Yes" to in this situation, she replied: *"I say 'yes' to parenthood, to family, to the ability to attain my desire. 'Yes' to struggling, to uncertainty, to courage, to responsibility, to initiative, to love."* When asked by the coach what did she say "No" to, she said: *"To all the risks and things unknown, to others' opinions, to a life bereft of children, to fears, to passivity, to giving up, to despair."*

The values she connected with the most, from the foregoing list, were determination and despair. The coach and Noam decided to discuss the association between the two values. Noam described a pattern in which each time she feels a very deep sense of despair, she breaks out of that place through coping and by demonstrating determination. When asked *"Where do you encounter this pattern in your interaction with your child?"* her reply was that it occurs on those occasions where she encounters difficulties: she does not consult with others nor does she stop to think, but acts out of determination on her own. She claims that her child has adopted the same behavioral pattern. During the training session with Noam the coach worked on developing her ability to seek help and consult at those junctures where such consultation would be beneficial in order to improve matters for her child.

## The Home Mission

We will ask the parent-in-training to write down during the week at least two additional and different situations, in which he had interactions with his child; add them to the table and draft: the description of the situation, how he reacted, what he said "Yes" to (and to what value did he relate when saying that) and to what did he say "No" (and in relation to what value).[26]

## Summation for the Parent-in-Training

During the last few minutes of the encounter the parent-in-training will answer *Summation Questions for the Parent-in-Training*:[27]

- **What are your insights as a result of the encounter?**

---

26. See Navigation Sheet No. 14, p. 191.

27. See Navigation Sheet No. 2, p. 192.

- **Did anything strike you as particularly significant during the encounter?**
- **Is there any specific question you think I should have asked but didn't?**
- **Is there anything you would have done differently?**
- **Is there anything at all that you'd like to add?**

# Sixth Encounter

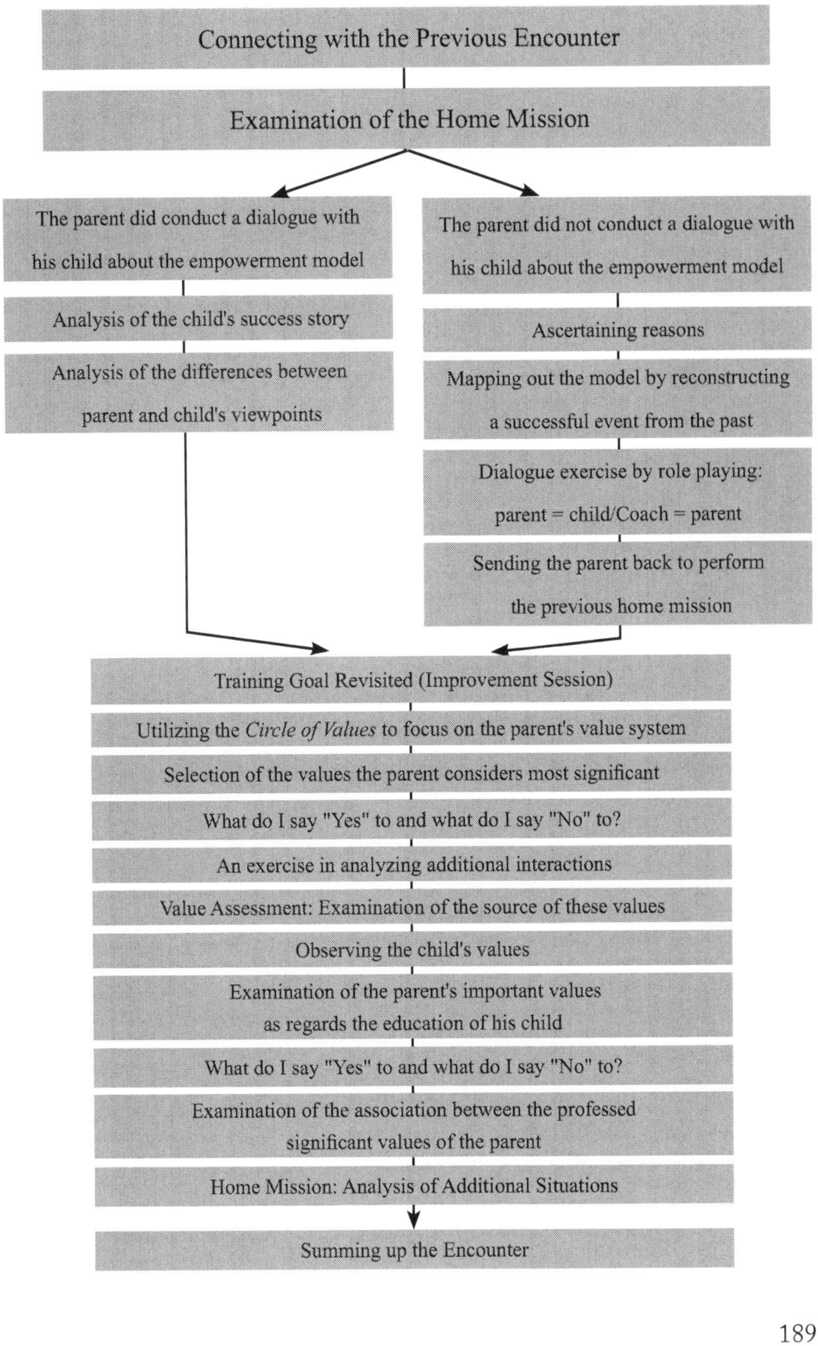

### Navigation Sheet No. 13 for the Parent-in-Training

## Circle of Values

### Which are the most important values to you?

Think about the seven most important values in your eyes. Then write them in the *Circle of Values*. Mark the two you consider the most significant.

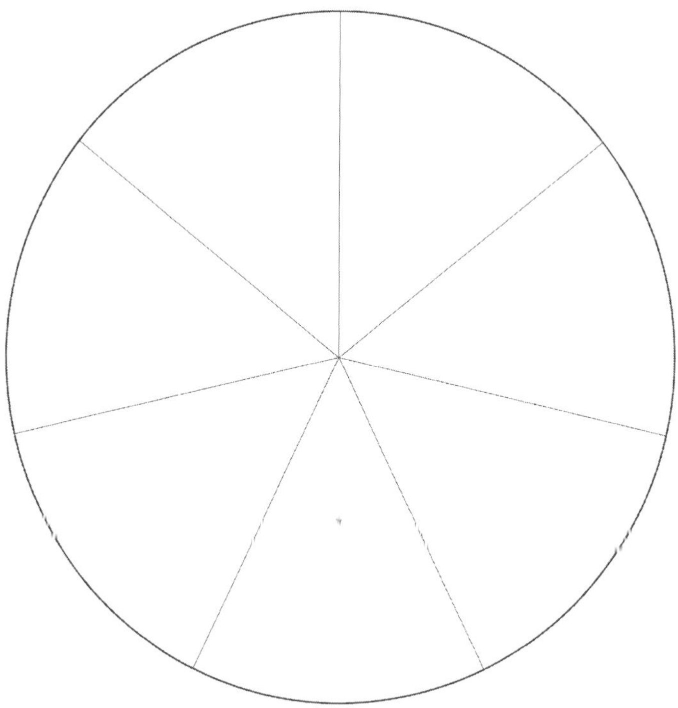

### Navigation Sheet No. 14 for the Parent-in-Training

## Typical Coping Accounts

Please describe certain interactions with your child and how you coped with them. Specify to what you said "Yes" and to what you said "No," and what was the particular value you related to in the process.

| **Description of the Interaction** |
|---|
| **My Response/Reaction** |
| **What did I say "Yes" to and what was the relevant value?** |
| **What did I say "No" to and what was the relevant value?** |

### Navigation Sheet No. 2 for the Coach

## Summation for the Parent-in-Training

During the final moments of the encounter, the parent-in-training will answer a set of questions; we will jot down his words:

What are your insights as a result of the encounter?

________________________________________

________________________________________

________________________________________

________________________________________

________________________________________

________________________________________

________________________________________

________________________________________

Did anything strike you as particularly significant during the encounter?

________________________________________

________________________________________

________________________________________

________________________________________

________________________________________

________________________________________

________________________________________

________________________________________

Is there any specific question you think I should have asked but didn't?

Is there anything you would have done differently?

Is there anything at all that you'd like to add?

## Seventh Encounter

# Assessment of the Advancement

We are past the middle point, and this is the time to assess the parent-in-training's progress. We will now go back to the future picture and ask him, how he sees his child from the present moment in time.

## Analysis of the Home Mission

At the conclusion of the previous encounter the parent was asked to bring additional examples of various situations taking place during the week in his interactions with his child. We will analyze these examples with the parent, focusing on the different aspects of the empowerment model: the strengths, weaknesses, threats, fears and opportunities. Next, we will examine which values of the parent-in-training and the child were manifested during these interactions.

We will utilize the following questions in order to facilitate the examination:

- **Please describe in detail what transpired there.**
- **What strengths manifested?**
- **What weaknesses materialized?**
- **What fears and threats were observed?**
- **Was there an opportunity present in the situation for you?**
- **What were the values that came into effect?**
- **What do you say "Yes" and what do you say "No" to?**

## Feedback about the Process

At this point the coach should describe to the parent-in-training the training process he underwent, to date. This description allows the parent to recognize the long road he has traversed.
The coach may say:
*"Till now we have been through a long journey, passing along some important milestones: We came to know each other, we discussed the future picture, we defined a training goal; we discussed strengths, weaknesses, threats, fears and opportunities; we talked about your values as a parent and we have created deeper awareness about various subjects. Today we are having our*

*seventh encounter, which is the time to examine where we are at in the process. We will do that using the future picture of your child."*
This encounter presents an opportunity for both the coach and the parent-in-training to assess the progress the parent has made during the previous six encounters, using the future picture he sees now.

## The Future Picture of the Child

We will ask the parent-in-training: **"How do you envision your child in the future? Describe this picture for me"**.[28] We will repeat the instructions provided during the second encounter: We will ask him to ponder for a few minutes, close his eyes, envision a future image from a virtual album, in as much detail as he possibly can. We then will ask: **"What do you see in that picture?"** We will use leading questions and ask him to describe a picture, not to tell a story.

## Focus & Clarity

When the parent-in-training tells stories and provides interpretations, he cannot connect with the picture and focus on its details. Such progress will be reached the more he notices, visually, the details that it is composed of. Progress will be achieved as he discerns the elements of which the picture is made.

28. See Navigation Sheet No. 15, p 211.

He adds colors, scents and emotions to the visual aspect, as it becomes tangible in his perception. The coach's role is to take the parent-in-training from the place where he tells a story to a place where he is able to visualize a focused, lucid picture: one that instructs him as to where he sees his child in the future.

In accomplishing that purpose, the coach may say: **"Please describe for me what you see in the picture, not as a story – but as a description."**
This time we will also add to the mix the values dimension and the empowerment model, and ask him:

- **What strengths does your child have?**
- **What are his values?**
- **What kind of a human being is he growing up to be?**

## The Future Picture From the Second Encounter

We will ask the parent-in-training whether he remembers the future picture he had described during the second encounter. We will ask him to repeat that description.
As part of the preparation for this encounter, the coach should go back and revisit the future picture of the parent, as it was presented by the parent during the second encounter. We will read, again,

thc description of that future picture, and remind ourselves what was said and the language used by the parent. If he does not remember the picture he depicted, we will remind him of his statements, but only after he has completed describing the current future picture.

## The Current Picture

The expectation is that by now the parent-in-training will describe a realistic yet optimistic future picture that is related to his child's strengths; that takes into account his weaknesses and limitations; and, that has in it all the components of the empowerment model as well as the values we dealt with during the previous encounters (one that gives a deeper, broader and more authentic expression to the approach leading the parent to see his child in the present). Such a future picture, which is at peace with reality, will allow us to incise from it the forthcoming tasks and applications.

## Comparing Pictures

The first future picture, described by the parent-in-training during the second encounter, marked the initiation moment of the process. Then the goal was to take the parent from an emotionally flooded place, to a different place – an optimistic one.

Now the expectation is transformed – that after the following process he has undergone to date, he can see the light at the end of the tunnel. He can see himself and his child on a different plateau.

We will ask the parent-in-training:

- **In what way does the future picture you see today differ from the one you saw during the second encounter?**
- **In the picture, what has changed as far as your child is concerned?**
- **Where is your child now?**
- **How does the picture differ regarding yourself?**
- **Where are you now?**
- **Is this your child's desire or your own dream?**
- **What do you feel when you look at the picture today?**
- **How does the process you've been through help you alter the picture?**
- **What contribution was made by (you becoming aware of) your child's viewpoint to how you see him now?**

We will then ask the parent-in-training to conceptualize the transformation with the following qucstion:
**"If you were to give this change a name, what would you call it?"**

## The Purpose of the Comparison

Analyzing the gap between the two pictures allows the coach to see the change that has occurred with the parent-in-training, to observe the extent of the shift in his experience. Analysis of both pictures allows the parent-in-training to find the golden path – to discover a point of balance – that gives expression to his strengths and values in his role as a parent: the strengths and values he wants to instill in his child, so that he will grow into an adult that stands on his own two feet and contributes to his social environment.

The comparison allows the parent to enhance his ability to conduct observations as well as his ability to conduct inner dialogue taking him beyond the 'here and now' mode of awareness, to one allowing him a vision of a future picture. When he can turn his vision to the realm of the future, new and additional opportunities unfold before him, providing him with tools to cope at a level he did not know previously. He ought to seal this visual depiction in his memory and from then on, constantly examine where he is in relation to what it presents. This picture is the vision that will accompany him all along the way to its fulfillment.

## Optimistic Picture:
## Inbal Sculpts

During the second encounter Irit was unable to decide at what age she saw her daughter till, finally, she said: *"She is twenty-six, surrounded by people and there is commotion all around her. She is smiling and happy. She and her friends are discussing what they are going to do that evening. As I see her, she's still a mess ... still not sure-footed about life ... this mess is somewhat typical of her."*

The vision Irit described during the seventh encounter was this: *"I see Inbal working at a large studio and she is sculpting; many materials all around her. She is thirty, wearing jeans and an undershirt, and there are several other individuals in the studio around her. These are customers who are examining the artwork, considering what they should buy, and there are some workers around, as well. She is so very content, and is giving instructions to the crew she employs. She is treating her employees kindly and respectfully. I come to visit her at the studio and she greets me."*

## From a Pessimistic Picture – to an Optimistic One:
## Nathaniel, a Lawyer

During the second encounter Avi found it very hard at first to envision a future picture of his son, Nathaniel. After a short while, however, he was able to arrive at a vision, yet it was very negative. To his mind's eye, *"Nathaniel is nineteen, a conscript in the army. He comes home and throws his gear on the floor. It would take a miracle for him to successfully complete his compulsory military service..."*

At the seventh encounter he said: *"I see a handsome young man, tall, wearing a button-down white shirt, properly ironed. He sits in an office and the sign outside the office bears his name. He is carrying a black leather briefcase; it is a moment before he leaves for court. He is surrounded by others and has a personal secretary. He is highly refined, educated and a scent of fine cologne wafts off him."*

## Same Future Picture

If the parent-in-training has stuck to the picture depicted in the past, we will seek to examine the differences between the two: **What has changed? How sure is the parent today about the future picture? And what makes him stick to it?** We will observe his conduct and expressions such as acceptance of (his perceived) reality, a sense of resignation, his body language, facial expressions and the like.

## Na'ama, a Shift Manager

Netta saw her thirteen-year-old daughter, Na'ama, when she was *"a twenty-three-year-old young adult, managing a shift in a photocopy shop, responsible for a small staff. She is very pleased. The managerial sphere of activity fits her well. She is both independent and sociable, surrounded by friends and contented with her share in life."*

During the seventh encounter, when she was asked once again to describe her daughter's future picture, she repeated the same depiction, but this time there was a difference in tiny nuances: in the tone she used, the certain, incontestable assertion that *"Na'ama can get there, her facial expression which radiated full faith and confidence."*

## The Aware Parent

The desired end is that at the conclusion of the encounter the parent-in-training will know to define and conceptualize the difference that has occurred in him and in his child. We will ask him: **What progress, in his opinion, did he make since the second encounter?**[29]

At this juncture, the expectation is that the parent will answer the inquiry from a place of awareness, after he had learned about himself and his child and following a dialogue he had conducted with him. The parent's understanding – that he is making progress and that today he is in a different place than he was when he started the process – is the fuel that will make him 'roll up his sleeves' and start exercising at The Gym – which is the next stage in the training process.

29. See Navigation Sheet No. 16, p. 213.

## Natalie's Advancement

When the coach asked Natalie what progress she has made since the second encounter, the latter replied: *"I am loading up the toolbox so that I can lead my family to a place of love, serenity, peace and comfort. I feel that today I have more tools and more awareness about ideas that I can implement. The understanding that amends can be made did not come too late. Today I can see the goal more clearly. I can see what I want to achieve and I am on my way there. It relates to self-fulfillment, both at home and with the children ... I am nearing this tranquility... the wondrous balance I am searching for."*

## Reinforcing Strengths

*"Now I can see her strengths, her dancing talent, and how she is able to set all the other girls in motion during the break. At first, the only thing I considered important was her academic success, and due to her difficulties I thought that, at most, she would be a minor clerk in an obscure office."*

## Preparation for the Action Stage

We will ask the parent-in-training to go back to different situations he had with his child out of the examples he brought up during the previous encounters. We will then ask him to choose one mission – a particular situation where he experiences difficulties with his child. This mission should advance him to the place where he wants to take his child in order to serve the future picture he had described during the last encounter.

It is important to insure that the mission is tied with the current picture of the parent in relation to his child, and to the entire process he has been through so far.

We will assist him to choose the mission and ask: **"What are you doing today in order to assist your child to be in this place?"**

## The Home Mission: Mission Construction

Choosing the mission, its planning and assessment are of the utmost importance and these should be engaged in before its execution in the field. Often, the parent-in-training repeats particular habitual behaviors and reactions out of habit, which lead to the same undesired results. The coach will ask him, at the training room, to stop, think, analyze and assess his actions. Accordingly, at this stage, the parent should think about the mission he had picked and to construct it in accord with the coach's instructions.

It is imperative that the training mission be measurable. A mission that cannot be measured is not a valid training mission, for the parent won't be able to ascertain the progress he is making.

The parent will be asked to answer the following

questions:[30]

- **Please provide a description of the mission you have opted to perform.**
- **How do you intend to act?**
- **How does the chosen mission serve the future picture?**
- **Who would you have to participate in bringing the mission into effect?**
- **Who could assist you in performing the mission?**

## Riding a Bicycle

Sam described the future picture of his child as a successful businessman who is very sociable, too. In order to manifest his vision, he came to an awareness that the one thing his son needs the most is a reinforcement of his self-image/self-esteem, and that is what he wanted to teach and provide for his son.

Since embracing the self-image is crucial to the fulfillment of the future picture, he chose the mission of jointly riding a bicycle with his son. Its aim was to underscore the child's many talents and abilities, and via a dialogue with him, accord him positive reinforcement concerning his physical prowess, determination and perseverance.

30. See Navigation Sheet No. 17, p. 214.

## Art Instead of Math

Nira saw her daughter, Noa, as an artist working in a studio: presenting exhibitions, enjoying what she was doing and being successful. At present Noa is struggling with math and Nira sits with her for hours on end to assist her in closing the gap with other students in her class. The process was accompanied by many quarrels and a sense of missing opportunities. Following the training process the mother reached an awareness that she wants to promote her daughter where the latter has strengths. In order for Noa to become an artist in the future it would be important to dedicate, in the present, time to promote her fruition as an artist – even at the expense of math studies. In order to materialize the future vision she saw and develop her child's artistic talents, the mission the mother chose was going together to extracurricular painting classes so as to strengthen her daughter in a place where she could grow as she was enjoying herself.

## Honing the Training Mission in Before Departure for *The Gym*

Actually, till this stage, the coach and parent-in-training have examined, together, the evolution of the training goal, till achieving its final definition. It is essential that the parent reach a high degree of clarity and lucidity in regard to the goal, before going on to The Gym. He shall arrive there when he has become aware of his own hurdles as well as the opportunity coming his way for effective coping. The exercise in The Gym will assist him to internalize the change in his daily conduct.

## Summation for the Parent-in-Training

During the last few minutes of the encounter the parent-in-training will answer *Summation Questions for the Parent-in-Training*:[31]

- **What are your insights as a result of the encounter?**
- **Did anything strike you as particularly significant during the encounter?**
- **Is there any specific question you think I should have asked but didn't?**
- **Is there anything you would have done differently?**
- **Is there anything at all that you'd like to add?**

31. See Navigation Sheet No. 2, p. 216.

# Seventh Encounter

Opening and correlation with the previous encounter

Examination of the home mission

Review of the milestones of the training process

Describing a second future picture of the child

Adding the values' dimension and the empowerment model to the picture

Revisiting the future picture from the second encounter

Comparison between the two future pictures

Delineating the changes that occurred in both the parent and the child

Choosing a mission that brings the parent closer to the future picture

The home mission: Mission construction

Clarifying and elucidating the training mission before departing for The Gym

Summing up the encounter

### Navigation Sheet No. 15 for the Coach

## A Future Picture of the Child

We will ask the parent-in-training: "**How do you envision your child in the future? Describe a picture for me, please**." We will now repeat the instructions made at the second encounter. We will encourage him to describe a future image of his child, taken from a virtual album of a probable future, as detailed as possible. We will ask him to ponder for a few minutes, and then close his eyes and focus on the picture that rises in his mind's eye; we will ask him to describe a picture – not to tell a story. We will write his words.

### For example

I see my daughter sitting in the living room with friends. They are watching a movie; she is snuggled up in a blanket …

### Navigation Sheet No. 16 for the Coach

## The Aware Parent-in-Training

We will ask the parent-in-training: What progress, in your opinion, have you achieved since the second encounter?

We will jot down his words.

### Navigation Sheet No. 17 for the Parent-in-Training

## Construction of the Mission

In order to plan the mission you have chosen to perform answer the following questions:

Describe the mission you have chosen:

How do you intend to enact it?

How does the chosen mission serve the future picture?

Who would you have participate in bringing the mission into effect?

Who could assist you in performing the mission?

### Navigation Sheet No. 2 for the Coach

## Summation for the Parent-in-Training

During the final moments of the encounter, the parent-in-training will answer a set of questions; we will jot down his words:

What are your insights as a result of the encounter?

______________________________________________

______________________________________________

______________________________________________

______________________________________________

______________________________________________

______________________________________________

______________________________________________

______________________________________________

Did anything strike you as particularly significant during the encounter?

______________________________________________

______________________________________________

______________________________________________

______________________________________________

______________________________________________

______________________________________________

______________________________________________

______________________________________________

Is there any specific question you think I should have asked but didn't?

Is there anything you would have done differently?

Is there anything at all that you'd like to add?

## Eighth Encounter

# Preparing for *The Gym*

Till now, the parent-in-training went through the interrogation stage and has developed new insights that will allow him to operate at an optimal level as he moves toward achieving the training goal. The next four encounters will be dedicated to the attainment of the training goal; they will be devoted to the action stage, where the parent goes on selected missions. The goal is to put the parent through a process of reflection enabling him to examine the training goal, its clarity, its focus on the child and the child's strengths. The goal is to ascertain the parent's needs, his strengths and to what extent the mission assists in fulfillment of the child's future picture.

## The Rationale of The Gym

Initially, explain to the parent-in-training the rationale that guides the workout in The Gym. The process is circular: It starts with planning, continues with execution and is completed by doing an assessment.

The training purpose is to improve from one mission to the next, and to create a learning curve with which the parent's progress is measured as he progresses from mission to mission on the basis of the empowerment model, values and the future picture he had described.

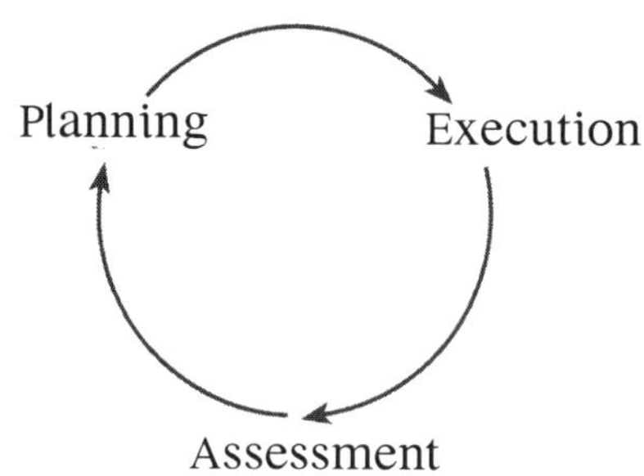


During the forthcoming encounters at The Gym, each mission will be put through an identical process of planning, execution and assessment. In the training room we discuss the mission with the parent-in-training, draw the requisite lessons from the manner of its performance and determine how we will work its implementation during the succeeding mission. After assessment the coach and the parent, once more, arrive at the planning stage as they spiral to the next mission.

The Gym serves as a work tool for the parent-in-training and it will continue to serve him long after the training will have come to an end.

## Reviewing the Home Mission

Within the framework of the home mission of the previous encounter, the parent-in-training was asked to choose a training mission. At the start of this encounter, the coach and parent should analyze the chosen mission, and then plan it together in minute detail. The aim is to enable the parent a reflective process where he will examine the training mission, its clarity, its focus on his and the child's needs and strengths, and to ascertain the degree to which the mission is a direct outcome of the future picture of his child, the empowerment model and the values the parent desires to instill in his child.

## Queries

In choosing and planning the missions, we recommended arranging in front of the parent-in-training the future picture, his and his child's empowerment models and the circle of values he desires to impart to his child.

It is the coach's role to query the parent in such a

way so as to insure that the mission does fit the parent-in-training and his child:[32]

Designed to match the child's needs:

- **To what extent does the mission fit the child's strengths?**
- **To what extent does the mission take the child's weaknesses into consideration?**

Designed to match the parent's needs:

- **How does the mission suit the values that you as a parent wish to inspire in your child?**
- **To what extent does the mission take your strengths and weaknesses into consideration?**
- **What do you expect to see once the mission has been completed?**

## Moty & Hadas at the Bowling Alley

Moty wants to improve his relationship with his daughter, Hadas, thus he picked the mission of bowling together. The coach accompanied him during the planning stage of the mission, which was done in minute detail: Moty would ask Hadas to go bowling on the following Friday but would also inquire whether she had a different idea for their

32. See Navigation Sheet No.18, p. 233.

joint outing. When Moty was asked whether the mission was adjusted to his daughter's stumbling blocks, he replied: *"It takes into account Hadas's difficulty in entering a new social environment and that she is more comfortable in a one-on-one situation than in a big group. When there are too many individuals with us, she becomes tense, and sometimes responds with either a fight or a flight. It seems to me that it would be pleasant and not stressing for her that it will just be the two of us. It's not something we do every day … there are a lot of factors here: breaking the routine, combining playing into the event, and even an opportunity for teaching her new things. It also takes into account her strengths: cleverness, sensitivity and will power."* When the coach asked Moty if the mission was in harmony with his strengths as a parent, he answered: *"I do love bowling, so that in and of itself is sheer fun. We will create an atmosphere that will contain joy and pleasure, and I'm good at that. There is a realistic target here that I can meet. I'm good at securing cooperation, in organizing and in execution."* When they discussed past experience, he said: *"When Hadas was younger, I did things according to what suited me. I didn't think it out, completely; I just went with the flow of things. I didn't take into account her needs, and it often resulted in resentment and consequent quarrels. In planning this mission today, I'm trying to bring us closer by thinking ahead about what suits her, and put an emphasis on, mostly, closeness and encouragement: things she needs the most."* When the coach asked Moty what he would consider a success, he told her: *"I'll be pleased as punch if Hadas will cooperate and if we end up enjoying ourselves and, also, if we will be able to conduct a good and meaningful discussion."* The coach next asked what would help achieve success and Moty retorted: *"If a difficulty arises, then the thing to do is to avoid a sense of helplessness, because it affects her; to try to remember either success or a previous positive experience;" not to criticize or attack her. That, too, distresses her, even if she disagrees with me or opposes my wishes; and most importantly – to really try and listen, to listen all the way through..."*

## Implementation, Expansion, Going Deeper

We will assist the parent-in-training to implement what he has learned to date. We will take the advantage to deepen and widen the training in those areas where he has encountered difficulties – for example: to what extent did he underscore his child's participation in the mission?
We, therefore, will ask the parent-in-training the following questions:

- **How does this particular plan differ from the way you have acted previously?**
- **What are your insights from the training process?**
- **In what specific situations did you encounter difficulties?**
- **Was it problematic for you to define the mission? Please be specific as to why.**

- **Do you anticipate any hurdles in commencing the performance of the mission, its execution or its completion? Please describe such hurdles with as much specificity as you can.**

We will always remember to cherish the parent-in-training and encourage him at every step of progress he makes along the way.

## A Change Occurred in Moshe

When the coach asked Moshe how he acted in the past and how he acts these days, he said: *"In the past there was a lack of boundaries. I practically did not care when Arik came back home – as long as he didn't bother me. I only made a comment to him if it was an extremely late hour. I enabled all that. I understand that it was wrong. Now, it is going to be different. Implementation will be carried out after pondering it; it will be parenthood with a path and leadership."* When the coach proceeded to ask: *"What questions guide you as you choose to act in this fashion?"* he replied, *"How do I help Arik? How do I harness Arik to reduce resistance? What is most important for him at this moment?"* When the coach went on to inquire, *"What are your insights for the next mission?"* he responded: *"I have to have the same clarity I have at this stage of mission planning instead of speaking in generalities. It is important to enlist Arik to participate in the performance of the mission. It is a mission for both of us ... I have to do it within the dynamics of a dialogue and, in the process, diminish his resistance – for instance, during the weekend, when there is no particular activity (planned), to come home at 1.00 a.m.; when there are parties, concerts – he may come home at a later hour, as long as I know in advance where he will be, the time he is scheduled to come home, where he might spend the night … to allow him to bring friends for a sleepover after they have gone out together."*

## Empowering the Parent-in-Training

The training's ultimate end is to empower the parent-in-training, to awaken in him faith in his abilities, to strengthen his sense of being able to do and to accomplish. We will revisit previous encounters that have dealt with his strengths and weaknesses (commencing with the Fifth Encounter) and import from their strengths, from other areas of his life and past success experiences. In line with that, we then will ask him: of all his past successes, which could he incorporate into the mission at hand, and how?

## Success Begets Success

We will first define what would be considered a success and then examine its dimensions, i.e., to what degree would that success have an effect on other areas of life? We will aid the parent-in-training to broaden his observation ability so that he can consider even a minor success a way by which he can ignite other and further successes, each of which sparks and bolsters the one that follows. The coach will aim a spotlight on the subject of success, will illuminate the way it was achieved, will determine what the parent sees – and what the child considers – a success.

## Mission Redefinition

After the process of going over the mission analysis with the parent-in-training, it is possible that certain aspects of the mission planning will be altered. Thus the two should go back to the Mission Construction form and fill it out again, before going on to the mission:[33]

- **Please provide a description of the mission you have opted to perform.**
- **How do you intend to act?**
- **How does the chosen mission serve the future picture?**
- **Who would you have participate in bringing the mission into effect?**
- **Who could assist you in performing the mission?**

We should remember that the chosen mission must be focused and measureable.

33. See Navigation Sheet No.19, p. 235.

## Avoiding Frustration

We will explain to the parent-in-training that in order to succeed in the realization of the mission, he must assure that it will be pleasurable and dynamic; in other words, that it should not be either too easy or too difficult, that it will not be frustrating, that on one hand it will be challenging and on the other a fun experience. It is recommended to choose a mission that has a high probability of success, in order to energize his motivation to proceed and persevere. Thus, we will pick a simple, focused and manageable mission, avoiding a grandiose and complex one.

## Learning From Implementation

This encounter is the beginning of the activities at The Gym, for without implementation there is no learning. By training and practice, which will take place during the next few encounters, the coach will seek to fortify the learning method of the parent-in-training, in order to effect its absorption and implementation by the parent in new and additional situations in his life. The expectation is that from one mission to the next, the parent-in-training will learn and improve his performance – a process that will continue after the end of training and will be examined six months after its completion.

Small success leads to further success. We bring optimism, hope and the experiencing of success into the process of training. We endeavor to create a change: instead of helplessness and repeated failures – to a place where we can start producing success and cooperation between the parent and his child. The coach enables the parent-in-training to discover the strengths, the energy and inspiration within himself so that he can carry out a parallel process with his child, where he will facilitate for his child the discovery of strength, energy and inspiration within.

## The Home Mission

## The Initial Mission

After planning the initial mission the parent-in-training should bring the child into the process of its performance. It is possible that, as it is routed through the child's perception, it will undergo some change. The idea is the formation of a dialogue with the child in such a way that the mission will be challenging for the child as well as the parent. We will make it clear to the parent that following the discussion with his child, he is expected to commence execution of the mission. We will ask the parent to document all that transpired in that process and then answer the following questions:[34]

- **Describe the mission and how you have just performed.**

34. See Navigation Sheet No. 20, p. 237.

- **Who did you choose to participate in the mission?**
- **Who assisted you?**
- **How did the mission help with the manifestation of the future picture?**
- **To what degree did the mission match the strengths of your child?**
- **To what degree did the mission take into consideration your child's weaknesses?**
- **How did the mission connect with values you desire to instill in your child?**
- **To what degree did the mission match your strengths as a parent?**
- **What is your opinion about the manner in which you have acted?**

## From the Child's Viewpoint

We will explain to the parent-in-training that at the conclusion of each mission he will evaluate it from the child's viewpoint, as well. Accordingly, we will ask the parent to ascertain what his child experienced as the mission was carried out. We will offer him several questions he can use in that process:[35]

35. See Navigation Sheet No. 21, p. 241.

- **Did you enjoy doing what we did today?**
- **What did you enjoy? What did you like in particular?**
- **What did you find less appealing?**
- **If we were to do this mission again, what would you like to repeat and what would you have changed?**

## Summation for the Parent-in-Training

During the last few minutes of the encounter, the parent-in-training will answer *Summation Questions for the Parent-in-Training*:[36]

- **What are your insights as a result of the encounter?**
- **Did anything strike you as particularly significant during the encounter?**
- **Is there any specific question you think I should have asked but didn't?**
- **Is there anything you would have done differently?**
- **Is there anything at all that you'd like to add?**

36. See Navigation Sheet No. 2, p. 243.

# Eighth Encounter

Opening and Correlation with the Previous Encounter

The Rationale of The Gym

Examination of the Home Mission

Mission Planning: Expansion & Going Deeper

Empowering the Parent-in-Training and His Preparation for Performance of the Mission

Redefinition of the Chosen Mission

The Home Mission:

- Enlisting the child for performance of the mission
- Mission performance and its documentation
- Ascertaining the child's satisfaction

Summing Up the Encounter

### Navigation Sheet No. 18 for the Coach

## Queries

We will ask the parent-in-training the following questions and write down his words:

To what extent does the mission fit your child's strengths?

________________________________________________
________________________________________________
________________________________________________
________________________________________________
________________________________________________
________________________________________________
________________________________________________
________________________________________________

To what extent does the mission take the child's weaknesses into consideration?

________________________________________________
________________________________________________
________________________________________________
________________________________________________
________________________________________________
________________________________________________
________________________________________________
________________________________________________
________________________________________________

How does the mission suit the values that you as a parent wish to inspire in your child?

To what extent does the mission fit your strengths?

What are your expectations, once the mission has been completed?

### Navigation Sheet No. 19 for the Coach

## Constructing the Mission

After analyzing the mission at the training room it may be that the mission was altered. Accordingly, we will ask the parent-in-training the following questions and write down his words:

Please provide a description of the mission you have opted to perform.

How do you intend to act?

How does the chosen mission serve the future picture?

Who would you have participate in bringing the mission into effect?

Who could assist you in performing the mission?

### Navigation Sheet No. 20 for the Parent-in-Training

## The Home Mission
## The Initial Mission

Document the mission performance and answer the following questions:

Describe the mission and how you performed.

Who did you choose to participate in the mission?

Who assisted you?

How did the mission help with the manifestation of the future picture?

To what degree did the mission match the strengths of your child?

To what degree did the mission take into consideration your child's weaknesses?

How did the mission connect with values you desire to instill in your child?

To what degree did the mission match your strengths?

What is your opinion about the manner in which you have acted?

### Navigation Sheet No. 21 for the Parent-in-Training

## From the Child's Viewpoint

Ascertain with the child how he experienced the mission and write down his words.

Did you enjoy doing what we did today?

What did you enjoy? What did you like in particular?

What did you find less appealing?

If we were to do this mission again, what would you like to repeat and what would you have changed?

### Navigation Sheet No. 2 for the Coach

## Summation for the Parent-in-Training

During the final moments of the encounter, the parent-in-training will answer a set of questions; we will jot down his words:

What are your insights as a result of the encounter?

Did anything strike you as particularly significant during the encounter?

Is there any specific question you think I should have asked but didn't?

Is there anything you would have done differently?

Is there anything at all that you'd like to add?

## Ninth–Eleventh Encounters

# Training in The Gym

The next three encounters are training sessions where the parent-in-training undertakes the performance of additional missions and develops new and additional insights.

During each encounter an analysis of the previous mission and preparations for the next one will occur.

Each encounter will be composed of the following stages: planning, performance and learning improvement.

## *The Gym* Metaphor

There is a correlation between training the parent to training in The Gym, where a person builds up his muscles. He first arrives with no knowledge regarding the proper and effective way of working out, his muscles hurt and he starts to notice certain muscles which he did not use previously.

A personal trainer (the coach) helps him with building a personally customized training plan, accompanying him during training to insure that he exercises properly and takes what he has been taught so far into consideration. As the process progresses, the muscles ache less and less, the abilities expand and performance improves. The purpose of the training is that the parent shall come out of The Gym with the abilities he has acquired implanted in his awareness and that he is able to implement them in his daily interaction with his child, no longer needing personal accompaniment by the coach.

## Coherence Between Thoughts, Feelings & Action

The purpose of the encounters at The Gym is to form coherence within the parent-in-training. Coherence is, in this case, correlation between what one feels, what he thinks and the way he acts. Lack of correlation among these three will cause the parent-in-training to feel confused and frustrated.

For example: when one does something that he is not at peace with (might even be contrary to his values), one will feel a difficulty in performing the mission and might feel that it is forced upon him. If one understands what he is expected to do and why

– but feels that he lacks the tools to do the job – he experiences a sense of difficulty and feels frustrated.

## The Gap Between What Is and What Should Be

The coach's role is to notice what parts of the future picture had manifested in the mission's performance – and which did not. The gap between the desired result and the actual manifestation should be examined: the desired result is what I want to change. The actual manifestation consists of my activity patterns as a parent that preserve the status quo, thus not allowing me to generate a change.
The purpose of such examination is to bring the parent-in-training into awareness of his activities and to make him understand that his patterns of behavior prevent/block or, alternatively, promote the process of change.

## Understanding Difficulties and Ways of Action

Occasionally, lack of knowledge and the intricacy of understanding the disability block the parent-in-training from doing the right thing. For instance: a parent whose child suffers from ADHD, who expects his child to do his homework while sitting focused and attentive; or a parent whose child has difficulties adjusting socially, who expects his child to get along with other children during school breaks.

Sometimes the parent understands his child's difficulty (the 'why'), understands what should be done (the 'what') – but does not know how to act (the 'how'). The coach will assist him to focus on that link that requires insight, knowledge and means, so that he will cease doing more of the same. In other words, the coach assists the parent to understand that every once in a while he reacts in the same way to stimuli (behaviors of his child) – despite the fact that this way of (re)action does not achieve the positive results he expects. The parent-in-training has a behavioral pattern that has been set over the years (a classic form of conditioning) and he no longer seeks to develop new, effective reactions.

## The Measure of Progress

The measure of progress in the process depends on the extent that the steps undertaken by the parent tally with his child's ability to accept such steps. If the parent advances too fast, the child remains behind. The parent-in-training learns how to operate in harmony with the child's strengths and weaknesses; he learns when the child needs a 'strong' parent and when he might need a 'weak' one – one who is able to express his feelings and apprehensions.

At The Gym the parent-in-training moves from the intuitive stage – that is, the path where he had acted reflexively, not planning – to the stage where he reflects cognitively on his activity: where he defines what he thinks and feels, dissecting the process he is in the midst of to its constituent elements and then constructs the mission fittingly for his child and himself. In order to gauge progress, the way the parent-in-training performed at the present is compared to the way he performed in the past.

In the training process the parent-in-training learns to be in sync with himself, his child, the family and the surroundings, while all these elements are functioning at their best and while complementing each other. This experience becomes powerful for him and keeps irrigating and fertilizing the training process even after its conclusion.

## The Three Gym Sessions Layout

The parent-in-training is asked to arrive at every encounter, after he has performed the mission he opted for during the previous encounter. In each gym encounter we will go over all the steps: planning, execution and learning refinement. Learning refinement will be done as we analyze the mission performance. This will include its success or failure, analysis of the difficulties encountered, the child's reactions and the variance from the original plan, etc. As he returns from mission performance we will inquire of the parent:

**What are the reasons for success or lack thereof?**

We will relate to the course he traversed so far, to what he has learned and the insights he has acquired about himself and his child.

## Possible Scenarios

Experience teaches us that there are three probable scenarios:

1. The parent-in-training successfully performed the mission.
2. The parent-in-training performed the mission but was unsuccessful.
3. The parent-in-training did not perform the mission.

## The Parent-in-Training Performed the Mission Successfully

We will ask the parent-in-training to describe in precise detail how he performed the mission. We will listen to the description of the performance, reinforce him and compliment him for the progress he has made.

We will ask him to reiterate his commitment; that is, the guiding principle for constructing and performing the missions.

We will relate to every improvement – even the most minute he was able to accomplish – as if we had discovered a treasure. Occasionally, parents-in-training discount the little successes and fail to see the potential they embody. Thus, the "wow factor" by the coach underscores the 'small' detail the parent had overlooked and reflects to him the skill of observation, and discovery of the little accomplishments and the development of a positive approach, which eventually will lead to the ultimate goal expected.

## The Parent-in-Training Performed the Mission but Was Unsuccessful

Performance of the mission is not only measured by its success. It is also measured by the efforts the parent-in-training made and the insights he produced therefrom, which will serve him in planning the next one. Even if he comes back with a bitter feeling, with a sense of failure, the coach will place an emphasis and illuminate the good parts, the successful ones, in order to empower the parent and infuse in him strength so that he will not get discouraged and still be motivated to go on and to try again. The coach can underscore the effort the parent exerted and his will to succeed. It is important to hearten him by talking about his courage to seek the creation of something new, his willingness and the path already traveled.

We will ask the parent:

- **Despite the hardship you have experienced, what message have you conveyed to your child?**
- **What have you gained from the experience?**
- **What did your child gain from it?**
- **Was it really all purely a negative experience, or are there any positive aspects you can point out?**

## The Parent-in-Training Did Not Perform the Mission

If the parent-in-training did not perform the mission we will attempt to determine, in our discussion with him, the reasons that prevented him from its performance. We will utilize for that purpose missions he had performed in the past and analyze them in order to draw new insights, which could serve us in future missions.

## Tested by Results

Every mission, from which the parent-in-training returns, will be analyzed and summed up in accord with the result test – meaning, that the various aspects of the mission will be mapped according to the following criteria:[37]

- **Description of the mission**
- **Future picture: How do I see my child in the future?**
- **Awareness of strengths and weaknesses (The empowerment model)**
- **Values: What do I say "Yes" to and what do I say "No"?**

37. See Navigation Sheet No. 22, p. 264.

- **To what extent was the mission adjusted to the child?**
- **To what extent was the mission adjusted to the parent?**

## Sara & Hadas's Chocolate Cake

Sara imparted that she gave Hadas the book *Baking is a Piece of Cake* of the chef Karin Goren, out of which she could chose a recipe to her liking. Hadas picked a particularly easy one – Chocolate Cake for Beginners. All of the ingredients, except for chocolate, were already in stock at home. Hadas went to the grocery store and purchased baking chocolate on her own. Because she has difficulties with reading, she asked her brother to read the recipe for her. She invited a friend over, and working jointly, with Hadas overseeing the task performance, a party was had. Sara did not have the molds for 'English Cake,' which the recipe called for; instead, Hadas used the muffins' baking dish and watched the muffins as they baked. When they were ready, she gave everybody some. Performing the mission thrilled Hadas, the muffins were scrumptious and everybody praised her. She was ever so proud of herself! Time and again Sara emphatically spoke about Hadas's enthusiasm and the good mood she acquired as a result, the pleasant ambiance pervading the place as Hadas was making the cake, and Sara pointed out that she had a really fun time with her daughter. The coach and Sara sought to ascertain what the cause of these results was. Sara identified it: *"It was something that Hadas also enjoyed doing, something that was easy for her to cope with; an immediate product that was satisfying, an immediate positive reinforcement from significant people in Hadas's life. I think that I entered fewer confrontations with her ... in the past I would get hot under the collar and demonstrate to her my disappointment. These days I calm myself down and avoid displaying disappointment ... consequently, Hadas is less nervous. She accepts that we are her support system ... she wants to succeed and has acquired a better, more positive self-image."* Sara told the coach that after they were done baking, Hadas and her friend cleaned up the kitchen thoroughly – in contrast to Hadas's typical behavior – and then added, *"Hadas noticed that we want what's good for her. She even told me: 'How lucky I am that you care for me! I appreciate that a lot...' Deep inside she now respects us to a higher degree..."*

Sara had passed a message to her daughter that she could get along and be independent. Moreover, Sara learned that Hadas could succeed, that she has a managerial skill, initiative, drive, and that she knows how to supervise others kindly and pleasantly. Hadas also learned that it is not scary to try something new and she had the experience of a great success.

## Examining the Extent of Learning

In order to advance the process, the coach and the parent-in-training will examine the extent of learning accomplished from one mission to the next, by asking the following questions:[38]

- **How did you function previously, and how do you function now? What are you doing differently?**
- **Is there a difference, and if so, what is it?**
- **How do you explain the difference?**
- **What insights are you taking with you to the next mission?**

These questions allow the coach to emphasize those areas that remain unseen by the parent.

## Illustration of a Mission: Playing Monopoly

During the encounter, Orly chose as a mission: *"To sit and play a board game that requires thinking with Danni; I've never done it before with him."* When the coach asked her how that would serve the future picture, she answered: *"Both in the game and the future picture there are patience, love, lots of hugs and laughter. It seems to me that through the game we will generate quality time together, we will form closeness*

38. See Navigation Sheet No. 23, p. 266.

*and it will take some anger and stress off him. We will experience an interaction of a different kind, not the kind that's based on 'do's and don'ts.'"*

The assessment of the degree of correspondence between the mission and Orly and her son proceeded: *"This ties in for me with my empowerment model, because I use my intuition. I have chosen an activity that I can cope with physically, and also an area where I have control and knowledge of the rules of the game. I also devote resources, time and attention to the interaction – something that's not a given for me. I have to enlist peace of mind, leisure time, patience, to let go and not to insist, just to be together and have fun – those are the things I consider important. It ties in with Danni's empowerment model because, among his strengths there is a drive to succeed, and in a game that requires thinking there is the element of competition built-in, which will produce in him the motivation to play with me and win. I know that he loves games that have a challenge that requires thinking and which allows defeat of the other. He will feel confident playing a game he is familiar with, in which he has mastery and skill. The mission takes his shyness into account and it will be performed at home – where he feels safe. We will also choose a game he likes, and when he likes something, he has fun doing it. There is also an element of harmony in that we are doing something together; he always asks for such joint activity. The plan is to be at 'eye-level' with him – not to tower over him with instructions, creating a sense that I know how things ought to be done and he should acquiesce and obey."*

As the examination of the values that receive expression in the mission proceeded, Orly said: *"It ties in with values I want him to acquire: of love, cooperation, sharing, attentiveness, motivation to succeed and integrity. Usually, when playing with friends, he tries to cheat. I want us to say 'Yes' to integrity and 'No' to lying and cheating; 'Yes' to self-discipline, as he operates according to the rules in a mature fashion; 'Yes' to love, 'No' to power struggles between us; 'Yes' to joy and spontaneity and 'No' to stubbornness; 'Yes' to relaxation and ease and 'No' to stress, to being tough and to criticism."*

Orly was sent on her way to perform the mission with Danni. At the next encounter she entered the training room, a broad smile painting her face: *"It was fun and amazing yesterday, as we played together. We sat in the living room, just the two of us in the house. We laughed together, a lot. There was excitement and suspense – who'd make a better move, who'd win? It lasted two and a half hours..."*

Orly and the coach sought, together, to figure out in what ways Orly's current course of action differed from her previous pattern of conduct. She said: *"Till now the relationship was that of reactions to what a moment brought. Things were never planned in advance. Mostly we interacted in the morning, remembering all the duties and chores we had failed to perform and therefore, pressure was tremendous. In the mornings no one has any time for anyone else. Everything pops up urgently and we handled it in an automatic mode, the way I habitually react. Naturally, Danni responded correspondingly, till we devolved to the level of threats, screams and crying. I used to make demands on him but now that has changed. Now there is plan-*

*ning; we have tools. The fact that I agreed to play with him is different than things used to be. They (members of the family) always ask me to play with them and I always turn them down with a 'No.' Just the fact that I said, 'Yes' and even more than that, that I demonstrated to him the initiative of the activity; he really loved that. I want to continue to play with my children. Through that I receive, as a matter of course, closeness and cooperation, which till now I tried to secure with force, by ordering them around – but failed.*

*"The mission helped me understand Danni better. Sometimes, as he played with his buddies, I stood by and saw how he cheats in order to win at any cost; yet when he played with me, he was not only honest, he, on his own accord, gave me money I was entitled to receive but had failed to notice, declining to take advantage of my inattention."*

When Orly was asked what she might have learned about her son, she said: *"When he is not afraid of being judged or criticized, he does want to be honest; and, the most important thing, I realized that he loves me."*

## Planning a New Mission

At the end of each mission, the coach should ask the parent-in-training what, to his mind, should be the next mission. Together, they will process the choice of the new mission and its construction:[39]

---

39. See Navigation Sheet No. 24, p. 268.

- **Please provide a description of the mission you have opted to perform.**
- **How do you intend to act?**
- **How does the chosen mission serve the future picture?**
- **Who would you have participate in bringing the mission into effect?**
- **Who could assist you in performing the mission?**
- **To what extent does the mission fit the child's strengths?**
- **To what extent does the mission take the child's weaknesses into consideration?**
- **How does the mission suit the values that you as a parent wish to inspire in your child?**
- **To what extent does the mission fit your strengths?**
- **What are your expectations, once the mission has been completed?**

## The Home Mission

The coach will ask the parent-in-training to get underway with another mission, at the end of which he should ask his child the following questions:[40]

---

40. See Navigation Sheet No. 25, p. 272.

- **Did you enjoy doing what we did today?**
- **What did you enjoy? What did you like in particular?**
- **What did you find less appealing?**
- **If we were to do this mission again, what would you like to repeat and what would you have changed?**

We will ask the parent to document all that had transpired in that process and bring with him the documentation to the next encounter:[41]

- **Describe the mission and how you have performed.**
- **Who did you choose to participate in the mission?**
- **Who assisted you?**
- **How did the mission help with the manifestation of the future picture?**
- **To what degree did the mission match the strengths of your child?**
- **To what degree did the mission take into consideration your child's weaknesses?**
- **How did the mission connect with values you desire to instill in your child?**

41. See Navigation Sheet No. 26, p. 274.

- **To what degree did the mission match your strengths?**
- **What is your opinion about the manner in which you acted?**

## Nearing the Point of Parting Ways

At the eleventh encounter the power of the training process begins to be felt and with it, hints of the forthcoming parting are intuited as well. The fact that the training is reaching an end creates at times a mutual feeling – by both the coach and the parent-in-training – that there is a need for one more encounter or one more mission before the process ends. This juncture, however – at the zenith of the process, where both feel uneasy about parting ways – is where preparation should commence in anticipation of the forthcoming completion.

## Summing up for the Parent-in-Training

During the last few minutes of the encounter the parent-in-training will answer *Summation Questions for the Parent-in-Training*:[42]

- **What are your insights as a result of the encounter?**
- **Did anything strike you as particularly significant during the encounter?**

42. See Navigation Sheet No. 2, p. 278.

- **Is there any specific question you think I should have asked but didn't?**
- **Is there anything you would have done differently?**
- **Is there anything at all that you'd like to add?**

## Feedback for the Coach

The training is a joint experiential journey for the coach and the parent-in-training. The coach, not unlike the parent, does not remain aloof or indifferent as a result of the journey he has just been through with the parent. In order for the coach to best prepare himself for summing things up for the parent-in-training at the final encounter, he should write down his reflections regarding the process he has been through, and also answer the following questions:[43]

- **What did you experience during the training process?**
- **What insights have you gained from the process?**
- **How did the parent-in-training affect you?**
- **What are you taking with you from this training process to the next?**

43. See Navigation Sheet No. 27 p. 280.

# Ninth-Eleventh Encounters

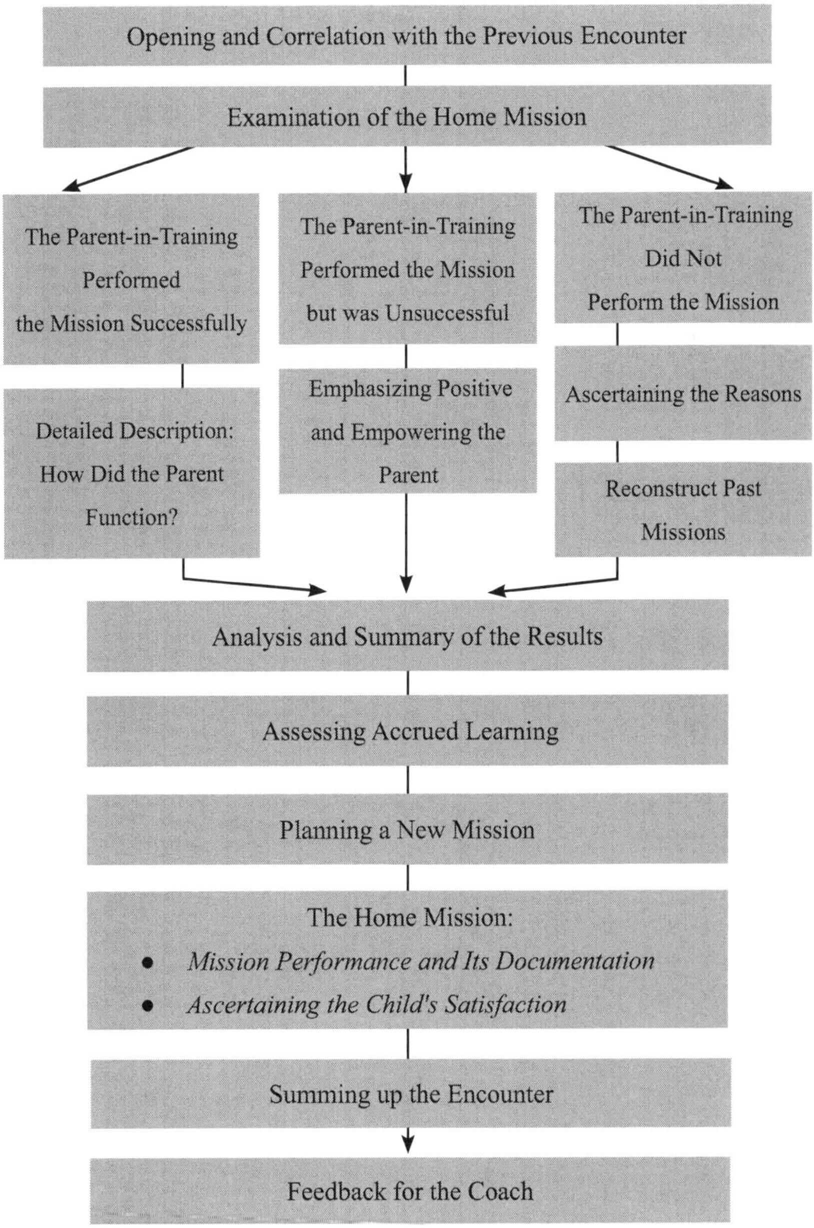

### Navigation Sheet No. 22 for the Coach

## Tested by Results

In every mission from which the parent-in-training returns, summary of the various aspects of the mission will be made in a succinct and focused manner in order to help the parent focus and advance to the next stage. We will write the parent-in-training's words.

| Aspects | What expression did these aspects have in the mission as it was being performed? |
|---|---|
| Mission Description | |
| Future picture | |
| Strengths | |

| Weaknesses | |
|---|---|
| Values | |
| Mission adjusted to the child | |
| Mission adjusted to the parent | |

### Navigation Sheet No. 23 for the Coach

## Examining the Extent of Learning

We will ask the parent-in-training the following questions and write down his words:

- How did you function previously and how do you function now? What are you doing differently?

- Is there a difference, and if so, what is it?

- How do you explain the difference?

- What insights are you taking with you to the next missions?

### Navigation Sheet No. 24 for the Coach

## Planning a Mission

At the end of each mission, the coach will plan the next mission with the parent-in-training. Together, they will choose a new mission as well as plan it. The coach will jot down the parent's words.

Please provide a description of the mission you have opted to perform.

How do you intend to perform it?

How does the chosen mission serve the future picture?

Who would you have participate in bringing the mission into effect?

Who could assist you in performing the mission?

To what extent does the mission fit the child's strengths?

To what extent does the mission take the child's weaknesses into consideration?

How does the mission suit the values that you as a parent wish to inspire in your child?

To what extent does the mission fit your strengths?

What are your expectations, once the mission has been completed?

### Navigation Sheet No. 25 for the Parent-in-Training

## From the Child's Viewpoint

Inquire with your child, how did he experience the mission? and jot down his words.

- Did you enjoy doing what we have done today?

- What did you enjoy? What did you like in particular?

- What did you find less appealing?

- If we were to do this mission again, what would you like to repeat and what would you have changed?

### Navigation Sheet No. 26 for the Parent-in-Training

## The Second Home Mission

We will ask the parent to document all that had transpired in that process and bring the documentation with him to the next encounter:

Describe the mission and how you performed.

Who did you have participate in the mission with you?

Who assisted you?

How did the mission contribute to manifesting the future picture?

To what degree did the mission match the strengths of your child?

To what degree did the mission take into consideration your child's weaknesses?

How did the mission connect with values you desire to instill in your child?

To what degree did the mission match your strengths?

What is your opinion about the way you have performed?

### Navigation Sheet No. 2 for the Coach

## Summary for the Parent-in-Training

We will ask the parent-in-training the following questions during the final few minutes and write down his words.

What are your insights as a result of the encounter?

_______________________________________________

_______________________________________________

_______________________________________________

_______________________________________________

_______________________________________________

_______________________________________________

_______________________________________________

_______________________________________________

_______________________________________________

Did anything strike you as particularly significant during the encounter?

_______________________________________________

_______________________________________________

_______________________________________________

_______________________________________________

_______________________________________________

_______________________________________________

_______________________________________________

_______________________________________________

Is there any specific question you think I should have asked but didn't?

Is there anything you would have done differently?

Is there anything at all that you'd like to add?

### Navigation Sheet No. 27 for the Coach

## Feedback for the Coach

In order for the coach to best prepare himself for summing matters up for the parent-in-training at the final encounter, we recommend that he write down his reflections regarding the process he has been through, and also answer the following questions:

What did you experience during the training process?

What insights have you gained from the process?

How did the parent-in-training affect you?

What are you taking with you from this training to the next?

## Twelfth Encounter

# Summing up the Process

This encounter is designed to summarize the training by taking a look at the significant events experienced by the parent-in-training: those which were powerful and effected a change.

At the start of the encounter the parent will undergo a reflective process that will allow him to look deeply into what he has been through so far, the progress he has made to date and his connection with the coach. At its conclusion, the coach will speak about what he has seen and experienced during the training and will end with words of farewell.

## A Significant Event

We will ask the parent-in-training to answer the following questions in writing – he will be provided with the requisite time in order to think it through before drafting his response:[44]

**"Of all the events that transpired during the various encounters, which of them do you feel was the most significant for you personally? Please describe the event: What took place? Who was involved? What was your reaction? Why was it significant for you?"**

We will explain to the parent-in-training that the question relates to a specific event, one that either occurred within the training framework or outside it; that this is not a general question that deals with the training at large. We will make sure not to ask leading questions, and therefore to avoid affecting the response with our words.

Next, we will examine the answer to the question. It is imperative to understand what has registered powerfully with the parent during the training process and what has brought up the change. The coach will try and understand what the turning point was for the parent-in-training, and will focus on it. It is crucial to shed light on that point in order to understand precisely what transpired there. This is the point of power for the parent-in-training; an apt metaphor would be a well where he goes to quench his thirst, i.e., when he experiences difficulty.

44. See Navigation Sheet No. 28, p. 300.

## Select Meaningful Events

### Closeness-Enhancing Communication With My Daughter

*"The simulation during the second encounter was the most significant for me. The home mission was to set a meeting with the child and talk with her, just the two of us, while employing communication that fosters closeness. In theory, it sounded great; however, I didn't know how one does it in practical terms. The situation reflected the gap I have been experiencing between the prescriptive and descriptive – between how I would've liked to communicate and how I do in fact. Accordingly, it was so important for me to perform the task. Till then, I did not notice... I was unaware of the shortcomings in our communication. Our assignment, to let go and to confer responsibility on the child, was very significant for me, and it seeps into my relationship with my husband and the other children. To tell you that it's perfect? We still have work to do, but that in and of itself was hard for me to do before and I didn't know how to do it. Today I know!"*

## To Stop Pretending

*"The moment I admitted my hard feelings toward my son, resulting from his behavior; the ability to bring it all out without apprehensions about being judged; to admit the existence of negative feelings in me, those of*

*fear and frustration; to expel the deepest trepidations that exist – that, as far as I'm concerned, was momentous! It is very important to me what others think about me and it was essential for me to be proud of my children, even show off – I painted a 'pink' picture, so dissimilar to reality. This awareness I've gained enables a change to the status quo. When I pretended, we did not tend to what had to be attended to. Today, I have already relinquished the game. That allows me to spend less energy (previously invested in upholding the pretense) and, instead, secure for him the help he needs, to bring us closer together and lessen the animosity. This awareness brings pain with it. You start to get used to the thought that it is going to be a long and arduous road. In the past I still entertained the hope that it would just be a passing phase."*

## A Safe Harbor

*"The encounter, where I had exposed a personal facet of myself, where I was able to express my feelings by crying; the fact that I allowed myself to cry and to accept that it is legitimate for me to feel and to express my feeling, that 'it's okay.' I got support and encouragement I was not familiar with till then. At that moment, this became the safest place on earth for me; it gave me feelings of inner peace and happiness."*

## A Heart to Heart

*"The encounter I had with Noa, sitting on her bed, was the first time I could actually hold a conversation with her and she, on her part, cooperated without any crying, without resisting, without bitter anger. This was the first time in years that she told me: 'Do you have any idea what a good mother you are and how much I love you?' She exposed her feelings both in words and by touch, and then we sat down and hugged each other. It is not possible to describe in words how touched I was. That encounter completely altered the relationship between us. It was a conversation between two good friends, and it has become a wonderful tool for me: one that avails heart to heart communication for us. It lets me understand, on one hand, what she thinks and what happens in school, and on the other hand, it gives me the opening for conveying messages to her and explaining things."*

## The Future Picture of Roy

*"At the encounter where I was asked to describe a future picture of Roy, I felt awful, a sense of vertigo. I had no picture in my head, save for a black splotch. I felt my brain as a disabled, rusty iron machine. The moment I could bring myself to saying something, I had this feeling of opening a door but only a tiny crack, yet I felt that something could open up in me. That was a meaningful event for me. Till then I could see nothing positive about Roy, his situation or mine."*

## Initiative at School

*"The most exciting and reinforcing experience I've had was the ability I've exhibited to take the initiative in relation to external factors and kick off a multi-team encounter at school, while I lead the ensuing discussion. Talking with the team members, I was able to change things around, and now Shirley – instead of being tagged there and marginalized – is getting attention and support. I arrived determined and with a meticulous plan, prepared for the meeting, and it worked!"*

## The Training Through the Eyes of the One Trained

We will conduct a dialogue with the parent-in-training regarding his feelings about the training process he has been through and his bond with the coach. We will ask:[45]

- **What did you experience during the training process?**
- **What are your insights as a result of the training process?**
- **What was the coach like for you?**
- **What would you like to express gratitude for, if anything?**

45. See Navigation Sheet No. 29, p. 302.

- **Is there anything you would have done differently?**

## Enlightening Spotlight

*"It all is associated for me with a spotlight. The first thing I experienced was that I shed light on the narrative only from my angle. That actual light should have been shed from several directions in order to see the whole picture. As a result of this insight the spotlight started revealing less accomplished sides of Adi – all of them, and me, as well. Before, I saw everything through the prism of problems; I turned everything into a problem. Now we are all privileged to be under the spotlight and receive (positive) attention."*

## Going Out As a Family

*"I have learned to trust and to know that there always is another side. I just have to look for it in order to find it. Now, my relationship is a million times better with other members of the household, and it is so much more at ease at home. My relationship with my husband underwent a magical transformation and today we're partners. I didn't train with my family, but I go out with family members … today I trust myself so much more and I'm fulfilling a dream – I am a college graduate student. I have been liberated!"*

## Rebuilding Myself

*"I now have more confidence. I am emotionally strength ened, less afraid of what might happen with Orr or that things might go out of control. I am so much more confident that Orr has the ability to succeed. I have learned to set boundaries and make demands. I am so much more authoritative. That notwithstanding, it is valuable for me to reach consensus. I have noticed that it works. I am better able to associate with my child. I need to draw much more strength for the long road ahead. He responds to the change in me … though it's not always easy for him … I learned that the emotional element was missing in my relationship with the children."*

*"The training process allowed me to rebuild myself anew, to alter behavioral patterns, to reach a place where I tell the child something – and he respects it. I have reacquired the parental authority [not a cliché, he indicates]. The process enabled understanding and the opening of a range of possibilities for activities. There is always more than one solution. Today I have more self-confidence. I feel emotionally reinforced, less afraid of what might happen or that things could go out of control."*

## Looking at the Full Glass

*"For me the training was a process of building confidence in myself, acquisition of tools for parental exercise; a place where I've opened Pandora boxes while with*

*the coach. I felt that I could share the difficult family accounts and receive her attention and understanding. It was both an emotional and cognitive experience. Today, I look at the full glass, at things that are better, reinforcing. The process has empowered me. It's really strange, but yes ... this empowerment comes from looking at things from a different point of departure, from a better place."*

## Faith & Strength

*"I leave the training with the journey notebook that accompanied me all along the way. This notebook is so precious to me. There are words in there that remain in my head, reverberating there... it helps me in moments of indecision and confusion. I then draw them out of the arsenal of memories. When the song,* Take Your Time Slowly *plays on the radio ... it helps me remember that things are well, that my child has his rate (of progress) and that's okay. Every time I recollect something from the training I tell myself that he will get along, that everything will turn out all right and it gives me strength and faith."*

## Fear Went to Sleep

*"Today I feel freer and more ready to take risks. When I first arrived (at training) I had many obstacles and difficulties with my self-management. Fear paralyzed me and I could not fathom what adventures I would embark on in this process, and what rewards and yields*

*I would reach. When I first arrived I felt that this was a golden opportunity, and that I could not get any lower. And you know what? Not only did I not crash, I have grown. During the last few weeks I feel differently: Stronger, more secure concerning my parental authority, and – finally – the fear went to sleep and I hope for a very long time.*

*"The training process has caused me to become aware of all that's happening around me: At work, at home, with my mate, and with my ex, Tsvika. Likewise, the training missions I was given expanded my awareness regarding all kinds of other processes, which, as I wrote things down, then I was inspired with solutions; for when I write I see things in black on white and it sharpens my concentration. I certainly will adopt this method in the future."*

## Bringing Order out of Disorder

*"I've waited like a little girl for the weekly encounters and the feedback I'd receive. The way you gave me feedback, with the warm smile, your eyes lit up and filled with faith in me, these were very important for me. I am departing with order made out of the disorder I had, with a better calibrated compass and with more comprehensible aims. I intend to hold on to the process I've been through and the insights I've gained, and to keep receiving guidance for assisstance, to develop and share – for I am not alone in this complicated campaign. I also want to commence another training process in a little while in the area of relationships with a mate,*

*but only after the processes I've been through will seep in and saturate my everyday life. I've learned that feedback may be had even for part of a mission/performance, and I'll take it with me into the process of raising my daughters."*

## Direction & Focus

*"The coach was in many ways a friend, except that she was much wiser than others ... one who directs, channels you, gets you back in order, straightens you out ... I came here and it was as if you reset me back at zero. I don't know if it was by design or not. I'm often scattered. Even when I ponder about Isaac, I worry about what could happen to him, what will happen to him, and this worrisome attitude bled through to the encounter, but the training directed and focused me."*

## Acceptance

*"Every mother is different, and no doubt I make mistakes. But I believe in what I'm doing. I do what I do because I do not know how to do it differently, and in that sense I feel that you accepted me as I am. You didn't tell me that I was wrong. That's me and that's my son, and the way we meet (as a result of the training), he and I, in order to make things better for us... it's something I did not encounter elsewhere, and yes, it was very helpful. Often professionals tell you what's needed and what's not. There are a lot of things that are hard to change in yourself. Here I felt that there was accept-*

*ance by you of me as I am, and these are my values and those are the things that are important to me, and others less, and we got along with all that and you have no criticism of any of it. We will learn, from all these data, to function in such a way that it will be better for my son and me."*

## To Touch Aches & Weaknesses

*"I'd like to thank you for the opportunity given me within the framework of the Nitzan Association to get into the thick of things, to touch the weaknesses and the aches, to dismantle patterns that block, which had me and my life stuck in a groove. I want to thank you for your patience toward and tolerance of me, your serious attitude, your strength, your power and your determination; for the fact that you didn't fall apart because of what I had to tell you and the hardship I shared with you; but most of all, I am grateful for the love and confidence I felt in each one of our encounters. I felt that you have so much love for me and for many others."*

## Order & Authority at Home

*"I think that if I had to start all over again, I would have started with those contents that burned up in me, and still they burn, which are order and authority at at home. I would reach a person like you, for only at a place devoid of judgment and criticism could I unload my stack. I was not afraid, at all.*

*"At the beginning, when you said that I was the one*

*who had the answers, I thought you were joking till you made it patently clear that you would not be the one who'd supply answers for me: that it was my role to dust things off. And, indeed, from one encounter to the next, I was strengthened, I checked, took risks … I, at first, did not believe I could do it but I found out that I have in me so much more than I believed; and most important: I've learned to love what is absent, too."*

## The Coach As a Significant Figure

*"During the twelve encounters you have become a most significant figure for me, as you accompanied me most hours of the day. You know what I feel toward you and how much strength it has given me during this period … I'll stay in touch, for you have been an anchor for me, someone to whom I could say anything and everything. I've felt that you have not even a drop of criticism or judgment; on the contrary, you have nothing but love and accommodation; and most important, you have enabled the enlargement of my insights."*

## The Change That Took Place

The reality with which the parent-in-training is coping, from an objective stance, did not change. The turning point is embodied in the area of the parent's interpretation of the reality and his ability to import the strengths and tools from the process he went through. In the absence of the physical presence of the coach down the road, the parent-in-training has to etch in his memory those empowering experiences, which gave him the strength and faith that he has the ability to successfully cope with his challenges.

## Part II: Training Seen Through the Coach's Eyes

The coach will describe to the parent-in-training his experiences and the feelings he had as a result of the process. In preparation, the coach will ask himself the following questions:

- **What did you experience during the training process?**
- **What meaning does the process have for you as a coach?**
- **What are your insights as a result of the training process?**
- **What was the parent-in-training like for you?**
- **What, if anything, would you like to express gratitude for and cherish?**

## From the Training

*"You were a partner along a road of learning and evolution. You have enabled me to be a partner in a process of observation and transformation, characterized by openness, authenticity and courage; to go on and believe*

*that we have a right to be satisfied and happy and to act toward achieving the same; to enhance my faith in the human ability to effect a change at every stage of his life; to observe and examine my life and my way of doing things; to go on and improve, to expand and adjust my parental abilities in accord with the changing age and needs for each child individually. You have enabled my propensity to cherish existing abilities: listening, openness, sensitivity, the ability to connect with the other and, together with him, undergo a process of empowerment, acceptance and lack of judgment."*

*"Your journey within, facing mine with myself, summoned for both of us a dynamic of growth and mutual learning. In this journey I, as a coach, have held a 'lamp' to light up the road for you, into the recesses of your inner being. Concurrently, I aim the 'lamp' inwardly, where I meet myself, so that I may learn and grow."*

*"You were a great person to train, with abilities and strengths, unique and extraordinary. You allowed me to accompany you with confidence along the path as a contributor and as a receiver of contributions. You are a strong woman. Your vitality taught me how to become stronger. Through you I have learned much about myself and thanks to you I, too, have grown."*

*"The manner by which you submitted to the training process has charmed me so much. During the encounters I've enjoyed, and was thrilled by, how articulate you are, by your need to be precise with your words and by*

*the authenticity with which you expressed your feelings. You were a fascinating partner in a process in which I trained and was trained."*

## Farewell

Despite the fact that the coach is a significant figure for the parent-in-training, without whom no change would have come into effect, the achievements are those of the parent-in-training. He is the one who generated the transformation and the tools he has acquired remain with him for further use. He no longer needs the coach in order to maintain the change that he has made, for his accomplishments have become second nature for him. With such words, the coach sustains and strengthens the parent-in-training and underscores his accomplishments.

We will conclude with a farewell. These are yours to say, and this is the unique way of each coach and each parent-in-training to come up with words of comfort, hope and love.

## The Twelfth Encounter

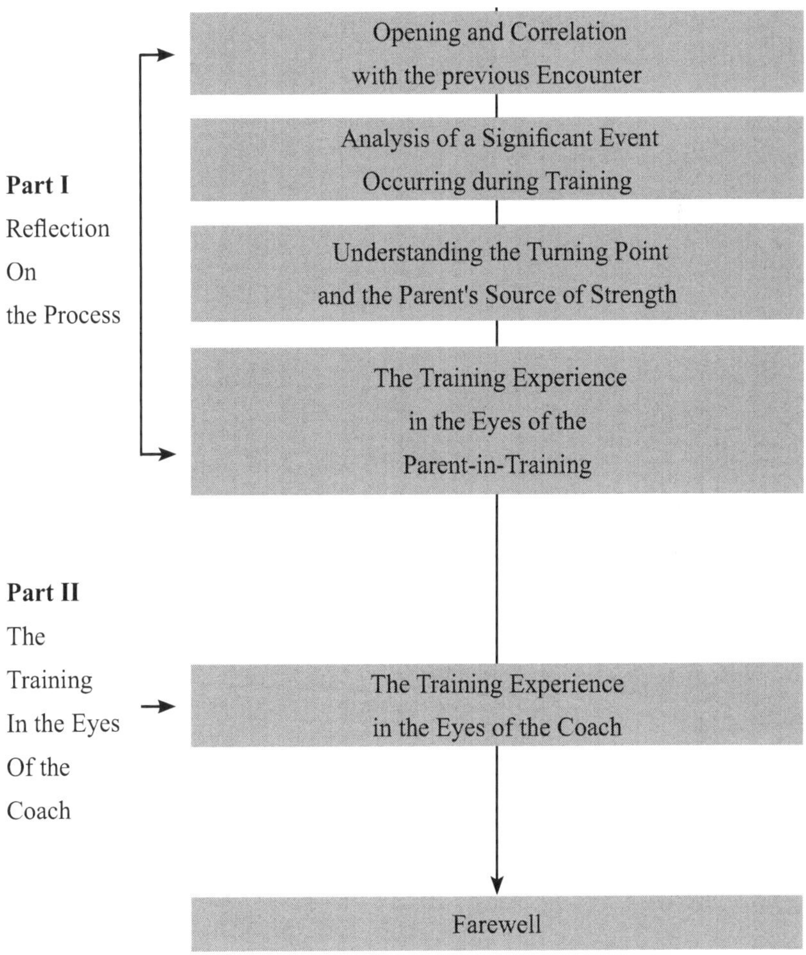

### Navigation Sheet No. 28 for the Parent-in-Training

## An Open Question

Please answer the following questions:
Of all the events that transpired during the various encounters, which of them do you feel was the most significant for you personally? Please describe the event: What took place? Who was involved? What was your reaction? Why was it significant for you?

- The question relates to a specific event occurring during training.

### Navigation Sheet No. 29 for the Coach

## The Training in the Eyes of the Parent-in-Training

We will hold a dialogue with the parent-in-training regarding the training process and his relationship with the coach. We will write down his words.

What did you experience during the training process?

________________________________________
________________________________________
________________________________________
________________________________________
________________________________________
________________________________________
________________________________________
________________________________________

What are your insights as a result of the training process?

________________________________________
________________________________________
________________________________________
________________________________________
________________________________________
________________________________________
________________________________________
________________________________________

What was the coach like for you?

What would you like to express gratitude for, if anything?

If you were to start the training over again, is there anything you would have done differently?

# Thirteenth Encounter

# Follow-up

The follow-up encounter takes place six months after the training process has reached its conclusion. During this encounter the coach and the parent-in-training will examine the training accomplishments from the perspective of the time that has passed since.

## Toward the Encounter

Prior to this encounter the coach should read all materials that accompanied the training sessions with the parent-in-training to refresh his memory as to the process they have been through.

## Assessing the Training Accomplishments Six Months Later

We will ask the parent-in-training what he went through since he completed his training, and examine with him the accomplishments of training six months later using the following questions:[46]

- **Where are you today? Where is the child?**
- **Where do you stand in relation to the training goal you have set for yourself?**
- **Does the process continue to occur after the training has ended? What have you preserved, and perhaps even improved, and what have you not been able to implement?**
- **What did you experience during the training process? What is the significance of the process for you with the perspective of time?**
- **What insights have you gained from the process?**
- **How did the training process contribute to your life: your relationship? Your parenthood? Your work?**
- **What do you need today?**

---

46. See Navigation Sheet 30, p. 317.

## Meeting Shula Six Months Later

Six months after training ended, the coach and Shula met again feeling thrilled and filled with anticipation. Shula said that many messages from the training are still reverberating in her head, and that she feels that a change came over her since the end of the process: *"I try hard to control my reactions ... I'm trying to be cognizant. Instead of giving him advice about how to do things, I'm trying to understand what he is going through, to give him opportunities to express his feelings ... I explain more. I'm no longer angry with him ... I now understand that he does not do things on purpose, that it's hard for him, emotionally, to control his reactions. Today I can allow Yoav more freedom, independence and room for decision-making. I let him handle the consequences of his actions. I think I'm less 'heavy' on him. I ask him and remind him about things, but I no longer open his school bag or put books and notebooks there for him. I stopped going over his notebooks – something I used to do all the time. He himself turns to me and asks,* 'I have a test coming. Will you help me?' *I also bestow on him the feeling that he can stay alone at home, that he is a big boy and he, too, feels this confidence. It is the same concerning the issue of inviting friends over. In the past he'd ask me to make the phone calls. These days I say,* 'He's your friend. You call. You know you can.' *Similarly, I used to coordinate rides to parties and birthday celebrations with other parents. These days I let him arrange it all.*

*I can hold on (and not do it myself). I do remind him, but I don't do it for him."*

Shula told about another event where Yoav was supposed to prepare for a test in Literature and said he was not able to do it. *"I asked him,* 'Can I help you?' *And, he replied:* 'You can't.' *I reminded myself not to pressure him. I let him experience the effect of his decision, and instead of saying that he must study and start making threats – that if he didn't study there wouldn't be access to either a computer or TV – which is what I would've done before, I just said:* 'If you have decided to give up, I accept your decision ... if you want me to tutor you, I'll do it gladly. If not, you're the one who'll have to deal with the consequences.' *To make a long story short, he passed the test. I can do it because I feel that he cares. I can let go because I see that it works ... if I had kept doing everything for him, he would have been constantly dependent on me... this way he is self-reliant ... Now he tells me,* 'Mom, come help me...' *That is truly a positive experience for me. In the past I felt that if I did not rescue him he'd drown, but now I know that he can swim ... I feel deep inside that he can."* Shula also said that his teacher reports a change in him at school: *"She says that he has greatly improved in his relationships with friends. She even called it "a radical shift." He is ready to interact and play with friends during breaks now. His friends accept him and there is a significant decline in the amount of confrontations with them. The teacher also said that Yoav had learned how to calm himself down much faster."*

Shula said she had gained many insights from the

process she's been through: *"I arrived with a desire for a quick, comprehensive and immediate change in Yoav, and every drawback reinforced in me my pessimism. Now I know that the change had to start with me, and that every struggle has its consequences in the future. Now, I am truly optimistic; I am filled with so many positive things! Sometimes when he regresses, I tell myself, 'His overall tendency is upward,' and I see that as what's salient. At home things are calmer. The flow is better and there are no arguments. That lack of communication and understanding has vanished. We've built a better relationship ... we've changed the approach and I am pleased with the way things have changed. The moment you adopt a different attitude it radiates on everything, even on my relationship with my mate. Before the training process, if something bothered me, I'd just explode. I couldn't at that instance see things from anyone else's point of view. Now I think to a greater degree before I take things out. I employ discretion and it sounds different. I come from a positive place. People understand you correctly when you come from such a place and they want to go through the change with you a lot more than when you come and cast things at people; then they become defensive ... at work, also, things have gone well ... I feel appreciated now. It's a good period in my life ... it's a good feeling to know that an essential change has occurred, and it's amazing to see how my change of attitude affected others' attitude toward Yoav."*

## Meeting with Avi Six Months Later

The coach was filled with anticipation toward the meeting with Avi and was curious to hear what had happened in his life during the period they did not meet. Avi, too, was easily excited about the reunion and indicated that he waited with bated breath to tell her what was happening at his place: *"I first came to training because I felt I had no bond with Shir, the way I'd hoped to have it. We had nothing in common, neither as far as areas of interests were concerned nor activities. What hurt me the most was that she was an outsider in the family: a younger sister to siblings who'd already left the nest, and there was a feeling that she was like a fifth wheel. Today, both Shir and I are at a totally different place. I now accept her exactly as she is and we have formed an excellent relationship. It's not like I submit to everything, but I less... ...I accept it. My level of anxiety has dropped and I'm more encouraging. I see my child from the angle of her strengths, abilities, and her force. I have let the matter drop. I have made peace with the fact that she will not attend extra-curricular classes and won't do too many things in the area of activity and movement that might be meaningful for me... slowly I've learned that as far as the 'big picture' is concerned, she is approaching life with an excellent 'payload' which, one of these days, will find an outlet. It was the training process that brought me face to face with this insight."*

Avi added that the training goals have remained

with him along the way: *"I think a lot about them. It's something that stays with me. I always see in front of my eyes her self-image, her family relationships, and her connection with me. It's in the air. I am aware and sensitized to it. Our communication improved. Today we can communicate without the presence of tension in the air – which once seemed impossible. The issue of values also remains present in my awareness, and it gives me parental confidence about what I do in that field. The way I, as a human being, process my priorities and Shir's values have lifted it all to another sphere. I feel more confident, stronger. My awareness and understanding that I actually am a good parent have become keener. I do not lose my temper as I once did. I'm calmer interacting with her, more attentive to her needs and to what's happening in her life today. For instance: On Saturday my wife and I returned from a trip down south to Eilat. It was hot there and we came back exhausted from the long drive. We just wanted to shower and hit the sack. As we opened the door there was Shir who said:* 'Dad, let's do something (together).' *I took her for a two hour outing at the mall. I was sensitive to her huge need to get out of the house, to how hard it was for her to stay at home all day long. This is something I wouldn't have done before. Today, simply put, I see her. Before the training I'd have said: 'Let her find, on her own, how to keep herself entertained,' and I'd go to bed for rest ... this time I said, it does not matter how tired I am – I'm taking the child out. I even went into a clothing store with her, even though it was of no interest to me personally. She wanted to show me a large and particularly interesting and unique store and I went in with her. Frankly, I remember nothing about the store, but she was thrilled. We went home, and it was obvious that that outing did so much good. Above and beyond that, today, I see her coping, but she expresses frustrations, also. For example, she got a low grade in Civics, went to see the teacher and talked to her, explained why she was entitled to a better grade. They had a quality conversation … She was accepted to an amazing high school, the best in our community, which is the one she wanted to attend. She was able to get in and become an architecture major. She is going there without most of her friends. They scattered to attend a number of other schools and she made the decision that she opted for change. She prepared very seriously for the entrance exam and her sister and I helped her prepare a folder of samples. She shares, she communicates, she initiates discussions and it makes me feel calm since I know that whatever bothers her, she brings it up and talks about it, and we iron it out...*

*These days, at school, she is preparing for the year-end pageant and they are preparing some sort of a dance. She tells us that all the boys want to dance with her, but she is kind of clumsy... At the ceremony (class graduation), I'll not see anyone else, only her and her dance. For me it will be absolutely perfect! What touches me the most is that a few days ago Shir said to me,* 'You know, Dad, you treat me nicely lately. In the past you used to be anxious, short; now you're patient with me.' *It's so much more pleasant – the relationship we have now – it creates serenity in my soul to know that co-existence is possible and present between us. I think my focus has shifted. I used to translate quality with a child based on a given model. Now I have moved to a different spot. I can see the qualities as I'm looking through an utterly different prism. I have tempered my judgment and criticism."*

It was important for Avi to tell the coach about what the family went through as a whole: *"Today the relationships with the siblings are excellent. The two older ones took our concern for Shir to heart, and moved forward with it. Today, Shir is glad when her sister comes for a visit. Her sister helps her with her homework, and shares with her. Shir now has a hold at home. Our son even asked if she would like to work with him on this year's Independence Day party, an event he organizes every year. He offered her the most responsible job: to collect money at the entrance!"*

In conclusion, Avi said that it is imperative to pass on the knowledge about the training to other parents: *"I think it's a very exclusive experience for parents. In a relatively short while you concurrently, put a great big focus on several planes in your life. The child is the excuse for doing it. You conduct some kind of a personal assessment, a process of raising consciousness, examining yourself as a human being, as a mate, as a parent – it's a process that awakens your mind to a lot of thinking and contemplation. You give things a definition and you take greater responsibility for your behavior, the commitments you have undertaken. If you care, you make sure to stand behind them. I arrived at the training rather skeptical. I'm skeptical about any kind of treatment, learning. You have to prove to me your knowledge and ability. Only then do I submit to the process. Now I see this training as a great gift I've given myself, in every which way. The process created a kind of encouragement. I could suddenly see Shir's strengths and abilities, the bonds in our family altered, and it helped me with the other children. One insight that came to light in my mind here is that if you just slightly alter the interpretation, you can stop being immobile; however, if you remain fixated on the same concept, statements, and mantra – it will all stay the same. The change that took place plainly concerns Shir, the other children and my wife, too. It's a process of elucidation, like a diamond that needed polishing, and that process and effect should be preserved. I always talk in platitudes about acceptance of that which is different. Here, however, I actually practice what I preach. It also now happens at work and most of all, in my relationship with my wife. Being different does not constitute a limitation, nor is it a handicap. Once this insight was a mere slogan; now it is a core belief in me.*

*"These days I give my thoughts a lot more weight. I assign it to maturity, age. I used to draw – like a Western gunslinger – I still do, but now it passes through a filter. I think things out. I feel really good about the new parts of self I've acquired. It is so much more pleasant to swim in this water, so much easier for me."*

At the end Avi thanked the coach for the encounter and told her she has been a very significant presence in his life: *"It feels good to talk about these matters after all this time, and also to hear myself the way I am today. It reflected to me the great progress I've made: indeed, a quantum leap. I live the change in my everyday life, and usually I don't pay attention to the fact that I deserve a "wow." Then suddenly I'm told, 'Look what you have achieved!' That empowers me a lot. I'd hoped that the vigor created by the training and my experience will not fade away, that it will be preserved, and I am so glad today that it has become part and parcel of my way of life. I see Shir now as she is and accept her as she is, and that's a lot. I no longer expect unrealistic things to occur and I'm no longer disappointed: that's my daughter – the same way I don't expect my wife to surprise me one morning with a beard on her face. I know that Shir is an amazing person, magical, even if sometimes irritating. Today there is acceptance. I am much more whole."*

# Thirteenth Encounter

Assessing the Training Accomplishments
Six Months Later

Where Are You Today? Where Is the Child?

Where Do You Stand in Relation to the Training Goal
You Have Set for Yourself?

Does The Process Continue to Occur after the Training
Has Ended? What Have You Preserved and Perhaps
Even Improved, and What Have You Not Been Able to
Implement?

What Did You Experience During the Training Process?
What Is the Significance of the Process
for You with the Perspective of Time?

What Insights Have You Gained from the Process?

How Did the Training Process Contribute to Your Life:
Your Relationship? Your Parenthood? Your Work?
What Do You Need Today?

### Navigation Sheet No. 30 for the Coach

## Experiences Since the End of Training

We will ask the parent-in-training what he went through since he completed his training, and we will examine with him the accomplishments of training six months later, using the following questions:

Where are you today? Where is the child?

________________________________________________

________________________________________________

________________________________________________

________________________________________________

________________________________________________

________________________________________________

________________________________________________

________________________________________________

Where do you stand in relation to the training goal you have set for yourself?

________________________________________________

________________________________________________

________________________________________________

________________________________________________

________________________________________________

________________________________________________

________________________________________________

Does the process continue to occur after the training has ended?

What have you preserved and perhaps even improved, and what have you not been able to implement?

What did you experience during the training process? What is the significance of the process for you with the perspective of time?

What insights have you gained from the process?

How did the training process contribute to your life: your relationship? Your parenthood? Your work? What do you need today

# Reference List

Anastopoulos, A. D., & Farley, S. E. (2003). A cognitive-behavioral training program for parents of children with attention-deficit/hyperactivity disorder. In A. E. Kazdin & J. R. Weisz (Eds.), *Evidence-based Psychotherapies for Children & Adolescents*, (pp. 187-203). New York, NY: Guilford Press.

Barkley, R. A., Fischer, M., Edelbrock, C., & Smallish, L. (1991). The adolescent outcome of hyperactive children diagnosed by research criteria: 3. Mother-child interactions, family conflicts & maternal psychopathology. *Journal of Child Psychology & Psychiatry & Allied Disciplines*, 32, 233-255.

Barkley, R. A., Guevremont, D. C., Anastopoulos, A. D., & Fletcher, K. E. (1992). A comparison of three family therapy programs for treating family conflicts inadolescents with attention-deficit hyperactivity disorder. *Journal of Counseling & Clinical Psychology*, 60, 3, 450-462.

Bender, W. N., & Wall, M. E. (1994). Social-emotional development of students with learning disabilities. *Learning Disabilities Quarterly*, 17, 323-341.

Beresford, B., Sloper, P., Baldwin, S. & Newman T. (1996). *What works in services for families with a disabled child?* Ilford, UK: Barnardo's.

Bérubé, M. (1996). *Life as we know it: A father, a family, & an exceptional child.* New York, NY: Pantheon.

Burlingame, G. M., Fuhriman, A. J., & Johnson, J. (2004). Process & outcome in group counseling & psychotherapy: A perspective. In J. L. DeLucia-Waack, D. A. Gerrity, C. R. Kalodner, & M. T. Riva (Eds.), *Handbook of Group Counseling & Psychotherapy,* (pp. 49–61). Thousand Oaks, CA: Sage.

Danino, M. (2007). *The parent as coach: Journey of a parent of a child with learning disabilities and/or ADHD. (In Hebrew) Rimonim Publishing.* (In collaboration with The Nitzan Association). Ramat Gan: Israel.

Danino, M. & Shechtman, Z. (2012). Superiority of group counseling to individual coaching for parents of children with learning disabilities. *Psychotherapy research: Journal of the Society for Psychotherapy Research*, 22(5), 592-603.

Denham, S. A, & Grout, L. (1992). Mothers' emotional expressiveness & coping: Relations with preschoolers' social-emotional competence. *Genetic, Social, & General Psychology Monographs,* 118, 75-101.

Doyle, J. S. (1999). *The business coach: A game plan for the new work environment.* New York, NY: John Wiley & Sons, Inc.

Dunst, C. J., Trivette, C. M., & Deal, A.G. (1994). *Supporting & strengthening families: Methods, strategies & practices.* Cambridge, MA: Brookline.

Dyson, L. L. (1996). The experiences of families of children with learning disabilities: Parental stress, family functioning, & sibling self-concept. *Journal of Learning Disabilities*, 29, 3, 280-286.

Greenberg, L. S. (2002). *Emotion-focused therapy: Coaching clients to work through their feelings.* Washington DC.: American Psychological Association.

Greenberg, L. S. & Safran, J. D. (1987). *Emotion in psychotherapy: Affect, cognition, & the process of change.* New York, NY: Guilford Press.

Hill, C. E., & O'Brien, K. M. (1999). *Helping skills facilitating exploration, insight, & action.* Washington D.C.: American Psychological Association.

Hill, C. E. (2005). Therapist techniques, client involvement, & the therapeutic relationship: Inextricably intertwined in the therapy process. *Psychotherapy: Theory, Research, Practice, Training*, 42, 431-442.

Holmes, S. E., Kivlighan, D. M., Jr. (2000). Comparison of therapeutic factors in group & individual treatment processes. *Journal of Counseling Psychology*, 47, 478-484.

Kaplan, H., Danino, M. (2002). Diversity as challenge and opportunity for growth in the school: Developing a caring community for students with learning disabilities. *The Educational Advisor, 11*, (pp. 64-87).

Kinlaw, D. C. (1999). *Coaching for commitment: Interpersonal strategies for obtaining superior performance from individuals & teams.* San Francisco, CA.: Jossey-Bass/Pfeiffer.

Koegel, R. L., Bimbela, A. & Schreibman, L. (1996). Collateral effects of parent training on family interactions. *Journal of Autism & Developmental Disorders*, 26, 347-359.

Margalit, M., Efrati, M., & Danino, M. (2002). Accommodation in matriculation exams for students with learning disabilities: A research and educational survey. *The Educational Advisor*, 11, pp. 48-63.

Miller, G. E, & Prinz, R. J. (1990). Enhancement of social learning family interventions for childhood conduct disorder. *Psychological Bulletin*.108(2), 291-307.

Shechtman, Z. & Birani-Nasaraladin, D. (2006). Treating mothers of aggressive children: A research study. *International Journal of Group Psychotherapy*, 56, 93-112.

Todd S., Shearn J., Beyer S., & Felce D. (1993). Careers in caring: The changing situations of parents caring for an offspring with learning difficulties. *Irish Journal of Psychology*, 14, 130, 153.

Valentine, D. P. (1993). Children with special needs: Sources of support & stress for families. *Journal of Social Work & Human Sexuality*, 8, 107–127.

Walker, J. M. T, Wilkins, A. S., Dallaire, J. R. Sandler, H. M. & Hoover-Dempsey, K. V.(2005). Parental Involvement: Model revision through scale development. *The Elementary School Journal*, 106(2), 85-106.